DAYS OF
DISCIPLESHIP

MANNY RIVERA

Cover Design: Cheyanna Rose Pelham

Print ISBN: 979-8-218-99174-6
Library of Congress Control Number: 2025927736

Table of Contents

Purpose of This Book

As pastors of Discover Life Church in Georgia, my wife, Victoria, and I have dedicated our lives to serving God and His people. Our journey in ministry has taken us through many seasons and places, from planting Impact Church in Miami to establishing Iglesia Vida Nueva in Clewiston, Florida. Throughout all these endeavors, one mission has remained at the heart of everything we do: DISCIPLESHIP.

In a world that often measures worth by achievements and accolades, it is crucial to redirect our focus toward cultivating a heart aligned with God's purposes. This devotional book is crafted to guide you into a deeper, more meaningful relationship with God, rooted in the principles of true discipleship as exemplified by Jesus Christ. The purpose of this book is to provide daily inspiration and guidance for those seeking to live a life of authentic faith. Each day's reading invites you to delve into essential themes of Christian living, challenging you to move beyond superficial faith into a transformative journey with Christ.

Discipleship, in its simplest form, is the art of discipline. It is about learning to walk closely with Christ, to grow in faith, and to live a life that reflects His teachings. Over the past 25 years, Victoria and I have developed a unique discipleship system called the Timothy Team. This program is more than a curriculum; it is a two-year journey designed to foster deep, personal growth in Christ, structured around four semesters of intensive, one-on-one mentoring and team-building. As Jesus taught in Matthew 16:24, "If anyone desires to come after Me, let him deny himself, and take up his cross, and follow Me." This call to discipleship is about embracing a life where we prioritize our relationship with God above all else.

The Timothy Team has been foundational in shaping the leaders within our churches. Many of the pastors serving at the churches we oversee began as members of this program, and nothing brings more joy to our hearts than seeing individuals transformed into committed disciples of Jesus. For us, discipleship is not just a part of ministry; it is the essence of our calling. As Jesus commanded, it is the work to which every believer is called: to make disciples of all nations. True discipleship is about nurturing an intimate relationship with God, marked by faithfulness, love, and a willingness to follow His path, even when it diverges from the world's expectations. This journey requires us to embrace the cost of discipleship, as highlighted in Luke 14:27, "And whoever does not bear his cross and come after Me cannot be My disciple."

This book is a guide for your own journey of discipleship. Over the next 52 days, you will be challenged, inspired, and encouraged to develop discipline in your walk with Christ. Through this book, you will explore what it means to carry your cross daily, choosing faithfulness over success and divine calling over personal ambition. Each day's reading offers a unique reflection, drawing from the core principles of our Timothy Team approach, such as the distinction between going to church and being the church or the difference between reformation and revival. As James 1:22 exhorts us, "But be doers of the word, and not hearers only, deceiving yourselves."

Each chapter is designed to challenge you to think deeply about your faith, inviting you to explore the rich tapestry of Christian teachings. To deepen engagement, each chapter concludes with challenge questions designed to inspire thoughtful reflection and practical application. These questions encourage you to consider how the day's teachings can be integrated into your daily life, allowing you to live out your faith with integrity and purpose. By confronting personal challenges and striving to embody Christian values, you can grow in spiritual maturity and understanding.

We invite you to dive deep into these daily devotions, reflect on the Scriptures, and embrace the process of becoming more like Christ. As you embark on this journey, remember that true discipleship is about transformation. It is about embracing the discipline required to walk closely with Jesus, denying yourself, taking up your cross daily, and following Him. This book aims to move you from passive faith to active discipleship, where your actions reflect the teachings of Christ.

In summary, this devotional's purpose is to guide you on a transformative journey of true, unadulterated discipleship. It invites you to engage deeply with Christ's teachings, reflect on your spiritual journey, and live out your faith with authenticity and conviction. May this book inspire and empower you to fulfill your calling, nurture your relationships, and make a meaningful impact as a devoted follower of Jesus Christ.

Enjoy the journey, and may your life be forever changed over the next 52 days.

Foreword

Pastor Manny Rivera is the first person who comes to mind when I think of discipleship . For over 20 years, I had the privilege of sitting under his leadership and mentorship. He's not just someone who teaches about following Jesus whole heartily, he embodies it. Now, as the Lead Pastor of Impact Church in Miami, Florida, I have the honor of continuing the ministry he birthed. His passion for discipleship has produced generational fruit.

52 Days of Discipleship reflects everything I've come to appreciate about Pastor Manny's approach to faith. It's practical, rooted in Scripture, and designed to challenge you. This challenge will take you from belief, to a faith that is lived out in a meaningful way. Inspired by the story of Nehemiah rebuilding the walls of Jerusalem in 52 days, this book offers a step-by-step guide to strengthening your relationship with God and embracing the transformative journey of discipleship. It is also full of what we in Miami call, "Gold Nuggets." Allow me to explain. A *gold nugget*, to me, is a powerful biblical principle or truth that carries immense value and practical worth for everyday life. It's a moment of divine revelation, a truth from Scripture that stands out like a rare treasure, offering insight, guidance, and spiritual enrichment. Just like a miner finding gold, discovering these principles feels like uncovering something precious. It's something that can change your perspective, deepen your faith, and guide your walk with Christ. A gold nugget isn't just knowledge, it's a truth you can hold onto and apply, bringing clarity and purpose to your spiritual journey.

What makes this book so powerful is how it combines gold nuggets, action, and faith. Each chapter encourages you to examine your heart, engage with God's Word, and take practical steps to grow spiritually. Whether you're new to the faith or have been walking with Christ for years, these 52 days are a roadmap to personal and spiritual growth.

For me, this isn't just a book, it's a continuation of the principles Pastor Manny instilled in my life. His guidance not only shaped my faith but prepared me for the calling I now walk in. This book captures the essence of that teaching, offering you the opportunity to experience the same transformative growth.

My advice? Don't just read through these pages. Sit with them. Pray through the Scriptures. Let the teachings challenge and refine you. Each day is an opportunity to lay another brick in the foundation of your faith, just as Nehemiah rebuilt the walls of Jerusalem.

From my heart to yours, I pray this book impacts your life as profoundly as Pastor Manny's ministry has impacted mine. This isn't just about reading, it's about transformation.

With gratitude,
Jonathan Olivardia
Lead Pastor, Impact Church
Miami, Florida

Dedication

This book is dedicated to my first "Timothy Teamers" in Miami. We started this in the year 2000. You know who you are. Keep serving our King by expanding His Kingdom. I'm so proud of all of you!

Why 52 Days?

The choice of 52 days for this devotional is not random; it carries profound biblical significance and a deliberate purpose that aligns with the heart of true discipleship. In biblical numerology, the number 52 is symbolic of transformation, renewal, and the establishment of something enduring and meaningful. This book is crafted to guide you through a journey of spiritual growth and transformation that will shape your walk with Christ in a powerful way.

The Biblical Significance of 52 Days

In the Bible, the number 52 is closely associated with the story of Nehemiah, who, against all odds, led the people of Jerusalem to rebuild the city's broken walls in just 52 days. This was no small feat; it was a monumental task that required unwavering faith, determination, and the united effort of the community. Despite the opposition, challenges, and setbacks they faced, the walls were completed in record time. The completion of the wall was a symbol of restoration, security, and new beginnings for God's people.

Just as Nehemiah and his people completed the rebuilding of Jerusalem's walls in 52 days, this devotional is designed to help you rebuild and fortify your spiritual life. It is an invitation to examine your heart, renew your mind, and strengthen your relationship with God over 52 days. Each day is an opportunity to lay another brick, to take another step toward spiritual wholeness and maturity, as you construct a life that is firmly rooted in Christ.

52 Days of Intentional Transformation

Discipleship is not a one-time event; it is a journey of intentional growth. Over 52 days, you will be encouraged to develop habits of prayer, study, reflection, and action that will deepen your faith and align your life with God's purposes. This period is long enough to form new habits and short enough to maintain focus and momentum. In just under two months, you will have the opportunity to break free from old patterns, establish new disciplines, and experience profound transformation in your walk with Christ.

Each day, you will engage with themes that challenge you to move beyond superficial faith and dive deeper into the heart of God. You will explore topics like the difference between going to church and being the church, understanding the cost of discipleship, and recognizing the value of faithfulness over worldly success. As you meditate on these truths, you will be building a spiritual foundation that can withstand the trials and temptations of life.

A Season of Renewal and Rebuilding

Just as Nehemiah called the people to rebuild the walls of Jerusalem, this book calls you to rebuild the spiritual walls of your life. The 52-day journey will help you identify the areas that need repair, whether it be a wavering faith, a lack of discipline, or a struggle with doubt and fear. Each day is an invitation to renew your commitment to Christ and to embrace the transformative power of true discipleship.

This process requires dedication, perseverance, and faith. As you progress through these 52 days, you will face challenges and moments of self-reflection, but you will also experience growth, renewal, and a deeper sense of God's presence. Just like the walls of Jerusalem, your spiritual life will be fortified, ready to withstand the pressures of the world, and equipped to shine the light of Christ.

The Power of Daily Discipline

Discipleship is the art of discipline, and it takes time to cultivate new habits and patterns that reflect the character of Christ. Science and psychology tell us that it takes approximately 21 to 66 days to form new habits, depending on their complexity. The 52-day framework sits right in the heart of this range, providing enough time for you to truly absorb and practice new spiritual disciplines while remaining focused and motivated.

Each day of this journey is a step toward developing the disciplines of prayer, study, reflection, service, and community that are the hallmarks of a mature disciple. By committing to these 52 days, you are committing to a season of growth that will extend far beyond this book. You are planting seeds that will bear fruit for the rest of your life.

An Encouragement to Keep Going

Remember, the journey of discipleship is not about perfection but about progress. There may be days when you feel like giving up, when the challenges seem too great, or the distractions too many. But know this: God is with you every step of the way, just as He was with Nehemiah and the people of Jerusalem. The 52 days will pass, but the impact of your commitment will endure.

Let each day be a reminder of the power of persistence and the promise of transformation. Trust that God is doing a great work in you, just as He did through Nehemiah. As Philippians 1:6 assures us, "He who began a good work in you will carry it on to completion until the day of Christ Jesus."

Embracing the Journey

As you embark on this 52-day journey, know that you are not alone. You are part of a community of believers, past and present, who have chosen to walk the path of discipleship with courage and commitment. This journey is not just about what you will learn or accomplish in 52 days; it is about who you will become—a devoted follower of Jesus Christ, rooted in His love, and committed to His purposes.

So, let these 52 days be a season of renewal, a time of rebuilding, and a period of profound spiritual growth. Let them be a testament to what God can do in a life fully surrendered to Him. May you find strength, encouragement, and joy in every step, knowing that God is at work in you, transforming you into the disciple He has called you to be.

Day 1:

Audience of One vs. Performance Mindset

In our service to God, it is easy to slip into a performance mindset, where our focus shifts from worshiping God to seeking human approval. When ministry becomes performance, the sanctuary transforms into a theater, the congregation becomes an audience, and worship turns into mere entertainment. In this environment, man's applause and approval become the measure of success, leading us away from genuine worship and toward superficiality.

The Danger of a Performance Mindset

The desire for recognition and validation from others drives a performance mindset. This mindset can infiltrate our worship, ministry, and daily lives, causing us to prioritize appearance over authenticity. Instead of focusing on God, we become preoccupied with how others perceive us. This shift in focus can lead to burnout, dissatisfaction, and a lack of spiritual depth. When we measure success by human standards, we lose sight of the true purpose of worship and service—to honor and glorify God.

The Consequences of Performance

When we approach worship and ministry with a performance mindset, several negative consequences can arise:

1. **Loss of Authenticity**: We become more concerned with how we appear to others than being genuine in our relationship with God.

2. **Disconnection from God**: Our focus on human approval can create a barrier between us and God, hindering our ability to experience His presence and guidance.

3. **Superficial Worship**: Worship becomes a show rather than a heartfelt expression of love and devotion to God.

4. **Spiritual Burnout**: Constantly striving for human approval can lead to exhaustion and disillusionment, as we are never delighted.

Scriptural Guidance

The Bible reminds us of the importance of serving God with sincerity and truth. Scripture consistently emphasizes that our actions and motivations should be rooted in our relationship with God rather than in seeking the praise of others.

Colossians 3:23-24 instructs us, "Whatever you do, work at it with all your heart, as working for the Lord, not for human masters, since you know that you will receive an inheritance from the Lord as a reward. It is the Lord Christ you are serving."

This passage highlights that God is our primary audience, not man. Our efforts should be directed toward pleasing Him rather than seeking human approval. Our true motivation should stem from our relationship with God, which brings eternal rewards and a deep sense of purpose.

Furthermore, **Matthew 6:1** warns, "Be careful not to practice your righteousness in front of others to be seen by them. If you do, you will have no reward from your Father in heaven."

This verse emphasizes the danger of performing acts of worship and service for the sake of being noticed by others, reminding us that true worship is a matter of the heart. When we focus on impressing people, we risk losing the genuine connection with God that comes from humility and authenticity.

Inspirational Insight

When we shift our focus to serving an Audience of One—God—our perspective on ministry changes, and our motivation becomes rooted in a desire to honor Him, not to receive praise from others. This mindset fosters genuine worship, allowing the Holy Spirit to work through us and impact those around us.

The Story of Mary and Martha

In the story of Mary and Martha, we see a vivid example of this principle. **Luke 10:41-42** records Jesus' words: "Martha, Martha, you are worried and upset about many things, but few things are needed—or indeed only one. Mary has chosen what is better, and it will not be taken away from her."

Mary's focus was on Jesus Himself, not on the tasks or performance, highlighting the importance of prioritizing His presence. This story encourages us to set aside distractions and to focus on our relationship with Christ above all else. Mary's choice exemplifies the heart of true worship—being present with God and valuing His presence above all.

The Heart of Worship

Focusing on God as our ultimate audience transforms our approach to worship and service. It invites us to seek His presence and guidance, allowing our actions to flow from a place of genuine devotion. This mindset shifts the emphasis from what we can achieve to what God can accomplish through us.

Application

Reflect on your motivations in ministry and worship. Are you seeking the approval of others, or is your heart genuinely focused on pleasing God? Consider how you can redirect your focus to an Audience of One, allowing His presence to guide your actions and intentions. Take time to examine your heart and ensure that your worship and service come from a place of genuine devotion.

Cultivating Humility and Authenticity

Strive to cultivate a mindset of humility and authenticity in your worship and service. This may involve setting aside time for personal reflection and prayer, seeking God's guidance, and asking for the Holy Spirit's help in maintaining a pure heart.

Prioritizing God's Presence

Make a conscious effort to prioritize God's presence over performance in your daily life and ministry. Create space for stillness and reflection, allowing yourself to be present with God and attuned to His voice. Embrace the simplicity of being with God and letting His Spirit lead you.

Challenge Questions

1. In what areas of your life or ministry do you find yourself seeking human approval over God's approval? How can you shift your focus back to serving God?

2. How can you cultivate a mindset that prioritizes God's presence over performance in your daily life and ministry?

3. Reflect on a time when you felt genuinely connected to God in worship or service. What elements contributed to that experience, and how can you incorporate them into your current practices?

By focusing on God as our ultimate audience, we allow our worship and service to become genuine expressions of love and devotion, free from the constraints of performance and human approval. Embrace the call to serve God with a pure heart, trusting that He will guide and empower you to fulfill His purposes with authenticity and grace.

Day 2:

The Closer We Get to the Cross

As we draw closer to the cross of Christ, we often find that the crowd around us begins to thin. This journey requires a deep commitment and understanding of the sacrifice and love that Jesus demonstrated. Reflecting on the ministry of Jesus, we see a pattern of diminishing numbers as the cost of discipleship becomes clearer. Jesus fed 5,000, but only 500 followed Him after lunch. He had 12 disciples, but only three went further into the garden, and only one stood with Him at the cross.

As T.F. Tenney observed, "The closer you get to the cross, the smaller the crowd becomes." This truth invites us to examine the depth of our own commitment to Christ.

Scriptural Guidance

The Bible provides insight into the cost of true discipleship. Following Jesus is not merely about experiencing miracles and blessings; it is about walking the path of sacrifice and self-denial. True discipleship involves carrying our cross daily and being willing to follow Jesus even when the road becomes difficult.

Luke 9:23-24 states, "Then he said to them all: 'Whoever wants to be my disciple must deny themselves and take up their cross daily and follow me. For whoever wants to save their life will lose it, but whoever loses their life for me will save it.'"

This passage calls us to a life of self-denial and dedication, reminding us that following Jesus requires sacrifice and perseverance. It is a call to put aside our own desires and embrace the path that God has laid out for us.

In the Garden of Gethsemane, we witness the dwindling support of even His closest followers.

Matthew 26:36-39 describes, "Then Jesus went with his disciples to a place called Gethsemane, and he said to them, 'Sit here while I go over there and pray.' He took Peter and the two sons of Zebedee along with him, and he began to be sorrowful and troubled."

This moment highlights the intimacy and vulnerability required to indeed follow Jesus to the cross, where few are willing to go. The disciples who stayed with Jesus in the garden were asked to watch and pray, but even they fell asleep, unable to fully grasp the gravity of the moment.

Inspirational Insight

The journey to the cross is a personal and often lonely path. It is easy to follow Jesus when it is convenient and famous, but it becomes more challenging as we draw nearer to the cross and the realities of His sacrifice become more apparent. This journey requires courage and a willingness to stand firm in faith, even when others fall away.

The apostle John is a poignant example of steadfast devotion.

John 19:25-27 records, "Near the cross of Jesus stood his mother, his mother's sister, Mary the wife of Clopas, and Mary Magdalene. When Jesus saw his mother there and the disciple whom he loved standing nearby, he said to her, 'Woman, here is your son,' and to the disciple, 'Here is your mother.' From that time on, this disciple took her into his home."

John's presence at the cross demonstrates a deep commitment to Jesus, even in His darkest hour. While others fled in fear, John remained faithful, showing the depth of his love and loyalty to Christ.

Choosing the Better Part

The story of Mary and Martha also illustrates the importance of prioritizing our relationship with Jesus over the distractions of life. While Martha was busy with tasks, Mary chose to sit at Jesus' feet and listen to His words.

Luke 10:41-42 records Jesus' response: "Martha, Martha, you are worried and upset about many things, but few things are needed—or indeed only one. Mary has chosen what is better, and it will not be taken away from her."

Mary's focus on Jesus Himself, rather than the tasks or performance, highlights the importance of prioritizing His presence. This story encourages us to set aside distractions and focus on our relationship with Christ above all else.

Application

Reflect on your own journey with Christ. Are you willing to move beyond the crowd and draw closer to the cross, even when it means standing alone? Consider what sacrifices you are eager to make to deepen your relationship with Him.

Seek Opportunities for Growth

Seek opportunities to grow in your faith and to support others in their journey to the cross. Engage in prayer, study the scriptures, and surround yourself with fellow believers who encourage and challenge you to remain faithful. By doing so, you can cultivate a community of support and accountability, helping you stay committed to the path of discipleship.

Embrace the Cost of Discipleship

Embrace the cost of discipleship, understanding that it involves sacrifice, perseverance, and a willingness to stand firm in faith. Reflect on the areas of your life where you may be holding back from fully embracing the sacrifice of the cross. Ask yourself what steps you can take to draw nearer to Christ and to align your life with His purposes.

Challenge Questions

1.   In what areas of your life are you holding back from fully embracing the sacrifice of the cross? Reflect on your priorities and consider how you can align them more closely with God's will.

2.   How can you take steps to draw nearer to Christ? Consider engaging in spiritual practices such as prayer, fasting, and studying the Bible to deepen your relationship with Him.

3.   How can you support others who are seeking to deepen their commitment to Christ, even when the journey becomes challenging? Look for opportunities to encourage and uplift those around you, offering support and accountability in their faith journey.

4.   Reflect on a time when you felt called to stand alone in your faith. How did that experience strengthen your relationship with Christ, and what did you learn from it? Consider how you can apply those lessons to your current circumstances.

By drawing closer to the cross, we embrace the actual cost of discipleship and experience the depth of Christ's love and sacrifice, transforming our lives and strengthening our faith. As we journey toward the cross, may we find the courage and commitment to stand firm in our devotion to Jesus, trusting that He will guide us every step of the way.

Day 3:

Success vs. Faithfulness

In a world that often measures worth by success and achievements, the Bible presents a different standard: faithfulness. God does not hold us responsible for worldly success but calls us to be faithful in all that we do. This perspective shifts our focus from seeking external validation to living a life that honors God with integrity and dedication.

Scriptural Guidance

The teachings of Jesus emphasize the importance of faithfulness over success. The parable of the Talents provides a powerful illustration of how God values faithfulness.

Matthew 25:21 recounts, "His master replied, 'Well done, good and faithful servant! You have been faithful with a few things; I will put you in charge of many things. Come and share your master's happiness!'"

This verse illustrates that God values our faithfulness in stewarding what He has entrusted to us, regardless of the outcome or recognition from others. It highlights that our faithfulness in little things can lead to greater responsibilities and blessings. The servant's reward is not based on the amount he has earned but on his faithfulness in using what he was given.

Furthermore, **1 Corinthians 4:2** states, "Now it is required that those who have been given a trust must prove faithful."

This passage reinforces that our primary responsibility is to be faithful in our actions and decisions, fulfilling the roles and tasks God has assigned us. Faithfulness is the measure by which God evaluates our service rather than our worldly achievements.

Inspirational Insight

God's measure of success is different from the world's. While society often prioritizes accomplishments, titles, and recognition, God looks at the heart. Our faithfulness in the small things reflects our trust and obedience to Him. It demonstrates our willingness to serve Him wholeheartedly, even when the results are not visible or celebrated by others.

The Heart of Faithfulness

Faithfulness involves a consistent and genuine commitment to God's purposes. It requires us to be diligent and trustworthy, knowing that our efforts matter to God even when they are not acknowledged by others. Faithfulness is about honoring God with our time, talents, and resources, recognizing that everything we have is a gift from Him.

In the end, when we stand before Jesus, He will not commend us for our earthly successes but for our faithfulness. As Jesus says in **Matthew 25:23**, "Well done, good and faithful servant!"

This affirmation highlights that God's approval is based on our consistent and genuine commitment to Him. It reminds us that our faithfulness is valuable and meaningful in His eyes.

Choosing Faithfulness Over Success

Choosing faithfulness over success requires a shift in perspective. It means focusing on what truly matters—our relationship with God and our service to others. Here are some ways to embrace faithfulness in our daily lives:

Prioritize Your Relationship with God

Spend time in prayer and study of the Scriptures, seeking to grow in your understanding of God's will. Allow His Word to guide your decisions and shape your character. Make your relationship with God the foundation of everything you do.

Proverbs 3:5-6 encourages us, "Trust in the Lord with all your heart and lean not on your own understanding; in all your ways submit to him, and he will make your paths straight."

By trusting in God and seeking His guidance, we can align our lives with His purposes and experience the peace that comes from living in His will.

Serve Others with Love and Humility

Look for opportunities to serve others, using your gifts and talents to bless those around you. Focus on meeting the needs of others rather than seeking recognition for yourself.

Philippians 2:3-4 instructs us, "Do nothing out of selfish ambition or vain conceit. Rather, in humility, value others above yourselves, not looking to your own interests but each of you to the interests of the others."

By serving others with love and humility, we reflect the heart of Christ and demonstrate our faithfulness to His calling.

Be Diligent and Trustworthy in Your Work

Approach your work with diligence and integrity, knowing that your efforts are valuable to God. Whether your tasks are big or small, do them with excellence and faithfulness, trusting that God sees and rewards your efforts.

Colossians 3:23-24 reminds us, "Whatever you do, work at it with all your heart, as working for the Lord, not for human masters, since you know that you will receive an inheritance from the Lord as a reward. It is the Lord Christ you are serving."

By working with diligence and integrity, we honor God and fulfill His purposes for our lives.

Application

Reflect on the areas of your life where you might be striving for success rather than faithfulness. How can you shift your focus to prioritize faithfulness in your relationship with God, your work, and your interactions with others? Consider how you can use your talents and resources to serve God and others to the best of your ability, trusting Him with the results.

Remember that God sees your efforts and your heart. Even when your work goes unnoticed or unappreciated by the world, your faithfulness is valuable and meaningful in His eyes.

Challenge Questions

1. In what areas of your life are you focused on success rather than faithfulness? Reflect on your priorities and consider how you can realign them to reflect God's values.

2. How can you encourage others to embrace faithfulness over success in their own lives and ministries? Look for opportunities to support and uplift those around you, helping them recognize the importance of faithfulness in their walk with God.

3. Reflect on a time when you chose faithfulness over success. What impact did that decision have on your relationship with God and others? Consider how you can apply those lessons to your current circumstances.

By prioritizing faithfulness, we align our lives with God's purposes and experience the joy and fulfillment that comes from serving Him wholeheartedly. As we seek to honor God with our faithfulness, may we find the strength and courage to remain steadfast in our commitment to Him, trusting that He will guide and bless our efforts for His glory.

Day 4:

The Goal of Discipleship is to be S.A.V.E.D.

Discipleship is the process of growing in our faith and becoming more like Jesus. It involves a lifelong journey of learning, transformation, and commitment. The acronym S.A.V.E.D. provides a helpful framework to understand the core elements of discipleship: **Scriptural Foundation, Authentic Relationships, Victorious Life, Engaged in Community,** and **Discipling Others.** These components guide us in our spiritual journey and help us fulfill our calling as followers of Christ.

Scriptural Foundation

The foundation of true discipleship is the Word of God. Scripture is the primary source of truth and guidance for believers. It equips us to navigate life's challenges, grow in wisdom, and align our lives with God's purposes.

2 Timothy 3:16-17 says, "All Scripture is God-breathed and is useful for teaching, rebuking, correcting and training in righteousness, so that the servant of God may be thoroughly equipped for every good work."

A solid understanding of Scripture is essential for spiritual growth. By regularly studying the Bible, we deepen our knowledge of God's character and His will for our lives. Scripture helps us discern truth from falsehood and provides the foundation for our faith and practice.

To strengthen our Scriptural foundation, we must prioritize time in God's Word, meditating on its truths and applying its teachings to our daily lives. This commitment allows us to grow in spiritual maturity and become more effective disciples of Christ.

Authentic Relationships

Authentic relationships are essential in discipleship. God designed us to live in community and to support one another in our spiritual journeys. Through genuine connections with others, we find encouragement, accountability, and love.

Hebrews 10:24-25 encourages us, "And let us consider how we may spur one another on toward love and good deeds, not giving up meeting together, as some are in the habit of doing, but encouraging one another—and all the more as you see the Day approaching."

In authentic relationships, we experience the love of Christ and have the opportunity to reflect His love to others. These relationships provide a safe space for us to share our struggles, celebrate our victories, and grow together in faith.

Building authentic relationships involves investing time and effort in getting to know others, listening with empathy, and offering support and encouragement. As we cultivate these connections, we create a strong network of believers who spur one another on toward spiritual growth and maturity.

Victorious Life

A victorious life in Christ is marked by spiritual maturity and overcoming the challenges of life through faith and reliance on God. It involves walking in the freedom and power that Christ provides, trusting Him in every circumstance.

1 John 5:4 tells us, "For everyone born of God overcomes the world. This is the victory that has overcome the world, even our faith."

Living victoriously means demonstrating Christ's peace and joy despite difficulties. It involves relying on God's strength rather than our own and trusting in His promises to guide and sustain us.

To live a victorious life, we must cultivate a strong faith rooted in our relationship with Christ. This involves prayer, worship, and a commitment to living according to God's Word. As we grow in our faith, we become more resilient in the face of challenges and better equipped to navigate the ups and downs of life.

Engaged in Community

Engaging in community involves active participation in the body of Christ. It means serving others, using our gifts, and contributing to the life of the church. As members of the church community, we are called to support one another and work together to fulfill the Great Commission.

1 Corinthians 12:27 reminds us, "Now you are the body of Christ, and each one of you is a part of it."

Being engaged in community involves recognizing that we are part of something larger than ourselves. We are called to serve and support one another, using our unique gifts and talents to build up the body of Christ and make a difference in the world.

To engage in community, we must be intentional about participating in church activities, serving in ministries, and building relationships with fellow believers. This active involvement allows us to grow in our faith and contribute to the mission of the church.

Discipling Others

Discipling others is a vital part of our calling as followers of Christ. It involves intentionally investing in the spiritual growth of others and helping them become mature disciples. Through discipling others, we multiply our impact and help others experience the transformative power of the Gospel.

Matthew 28:19-20 commands us, "Therefore go and make disciples of all nations, baptizing them in the name of the Father and of the Son and of the Holy Spirit, and teaching them to obey everything I have commanded you. And surely I am with you always, to the very end of the age."

Discipling others involves sharing our faith, teaching biblical truths, and providing guidance and support as others grow in their relationship with Christ. It requires a commitment to walking alongside others and helping them navigate their spiritual journeys.

To disciple others effectively, we must be willing to invest time and energy in building relationships, sharing our experiences, and providing encouragement and accountability. As we do so, we help others grow in their faith and fulfill their potential as disciples of Christ.

Challenge Questions

1. How can you strengthen your Scriptural foundation to deepen your faith and understanding of God's will? Consider setting aside dedicated time each day for Bible study and reflection.

2. In what ways can you build more authentic relationships within your community? Look for opportunities to connect with others, both within and outside of your church, and be intentional about fostering genuine relationships.

3. What steps can you take to live more victoriously in Christ, overcoming the challenges you face with faith? Reflect on the areas of your life where you need to rely more on God's strength and seek His guidance in overcoming obstacles.

4. How can you actively engage in your community, using your gifts to serve others and build up the body of Christ? Consider volunteering for a ministry or service project that aligns with your passions and skills.

5. Who are the people in your life that you can disciple, helping them grow in their faith and understanding of the Gospel? Identify individuals who may benefit from your guidance and support and seek opportunities to invest in their spiritual growth.

By focusing on being S.A.V.E.D., we align our lives with God's purposes and grow as disciples of Jesus, impacting the world around us for His glory. As we commit to this journey, may we find strength and encouragement in the knowledge that we are fulfilling God's calling and making a difference in the lives of others?

Day 5:

Going to Church vs. Being the Church

In today's fast-paced world, many people equate discipleship with merely attending church services. While going to church is essential, it is only one aspect of a vibrant spiritual life. The real challenge is to be the church—living out the teachings of Jesus in every aspect of our lives. Being in the church means embodying Christ's love and mission in our daily actions beyond the walls of the building where we gather to worship.

Going to Church

When you say that you go to church, it implies more than just attending a service. Here are some key elements that reflect a committed approach to attending church:

Consistent Attendance

Being part of a church community involves regular participation in worship and fellowship. Consistent attendance helps us grow spiritually and remain connected to the body of Christ. It is an opportunity to gather with fellow believers, worship God together, and be encouraged in our faith.

Hebrews 10:25 encourages us, "not giving up meeting together, as some are in the habit of doing, but encouraging one another—and all the more as you see the Day approaching."

Regular attendance allows us to be part of a supportive community that encourages us to live out our faith more effectively.

Serving Sacrificially

Serving others within the church is a reflection of Christ's love and humility. Sacrificial service involves using our gifts and time to support the needs of others. It is an expression of our commitment to following Jesus' example and living out His teachings.

Mark 10:45 states, "For even the Son of Man did not come to be served, but to serve, and to give his life as a ransom for many."

By serving sacrificially, we demonstrate our love for God and our willingness to put others before ourselves.

Giving Financially

Supporting the church financially is an act of worship and obedience. Financial giving supports the church's mission and demonstrates our trust in God's provision. It reflects our gratitude for God's blessings and our commitment to advancing His kingdom.

2 Corinthians 9:7 reminds us, "Each of you should give what you have decided in your heart to give, not reluctantly or under compulsion, for God loves a cheerful giver."

Through our giving, we contribute to the work of the church and enable it to fulfill its mission.

Loving Others Extravagantly

Jesus commanded us to love one another as He loved us. This love should be evident in our actions and attitudes toward others. Loving others extravagantly involves going beyond the minimum and extending grace, kindness, and compassion to everyone we encounter.

John 13:34-35 emphasizes, "A new command I give you: Love one another. As I have loved you, so you must love one another. By this, everyone will know that you are my disciples if you love one another."

Our love for others serves as a powerful testimony of our faith and our relationship with Jesus.

Honoring Spiritual Authority

Respecting and supporting church leaders is part of honoring God's established authority. By honoring spiritual authority, we demonstrate our commitment to the health and unity of the church community.

Hebrews 13:17 instructs us, "Have confidence in your leaders and submit to their authority because they keep watch over you as those who must give an account."

Supporting church leaders involves praying for them, encouraging them, and working together to advance the church's mission.

Being the Church

Being the church goes beyond mere attendance. It means embodying these principles daily, wherever you are. If we fail to do these things, we risk treating the church like a fast-food drive-thru—a place for quick spiritual fixes without steadfast commitment or transformation.

Being in the church involves living out our faith authentically and intentionally. It means being the hands and feet of Jesus in our communities, workplaces, and families. It requires us to carry the love and message of Christ into the world, making a tangible difference in the lives of those around us.

Application

Reflect on how you can move beyond simply going to church and focus on being the church in your daily life. How can you integrate worship, service, giving, love, and respect into your everyday interactions?

Living Out Worship

Worship is not limited to Sunday services; it is a lifestyle of honoring God in all we do. Consider how you can worship God through your work, relationships, and daily activities. Let your life be a testament to His glory and grace.

Serving with Intention

Look for opportunities to serve others in your community and beyond. Whether it's volunteering at a local shelter, helping a neighbor in need, or supporting a church ministry, let your service be a reflection of Christ's love and compassion.

Practicing Generosity

Be intentional about using your resources to bless others and support the work of the church. Consider how you can practice generosity in your everyday life, whether through financial giving, sharing your time, or using your talents to serve others.

Cultivating Relationships

Build authentic relationships with others, both within and outside of your church community. Be intentional about connecting with others, listening to their stories, and offering support and encouragement.

Honoring Leadership

Respect and support the leaders in your church and community. Pray for them, encourage them, and work together to advance the mission of the church. By honoring leadership, we contribute to the unity and health of the church body.

Challenge Questions

1. How consistent is your attendance at church, and how can you deepen your commitment to regular participation? Reflect on the importance of gathering with fellow believers and consider how you can prioritize this in your schedule.

2. In what ways are you serving sacrificially within your church and community? Consider how you can use your gifts and talents to meet the needs of others and demonstrate Christ's love.

3. How does your financial giving reflect your trust in God and support for the church's mission? Reflect on your attitude toward giving and consider how you can practice generosity more intentionally.

4. What actions can you take to love others extravagantly and authentically in your daily life? Consider how you can show kindness and compassion to those around you, reflecting the love of Christ.

5. How do you show honor and support for the spiritual authority in your church? Reflect on how you can pray for, encourage, and work alongside church leaders to advance God's kingdom.

By moving from merely attending church to being the church, we fulfill our calling as disciples of Christ, making His love and truth known to the world around us. Let us commit to living out our faith with authenticity, integrity, and love, embodying the teachings of Jesus in every aspect of our lives.

Day 6:

Reformation vs. Revival

In the Christian journey, reformation and revival are crucial processes that transform individuals and communities. While they are distinct, they work hand in hand to bring about lasting change. Reformation is often seen as the necessary foundation for revival, as a reformed mind is essential to sustain a revived heart. The relationship between the two is beautifully illustrated in Jesus' teaching: "New wine must be poured into new wineskins" (Luke 5:38). This emphasizes the need for transformation in both our thinking and our spirit.

Reformation

Reformation involves a thorough rethinking and restructuring of beliefs, values, and behaviors to align more closely with God's Word. It is about renewing our minds and aligning our lives with the truth of Scripture.

Romans 12:2 urges us, "Do not conform to the pattern of this world but be transformed by the renewing of your mind. Then you will be able to test and approve what God's will is—his good, pleasing, and perfect will."

Reformation requires us to examine our thoughts and actions critically, casting aside anything that does not reflect God's will. It often involves a deep commitment to study, prayer, and obedience to God's commands, leading to personal and communal change. This foundational transformation creates a new "wineskin" capable of holding the new wine of revival.

The Process of Reformation

Reformation is a process that involves several key elements:

1. **Renewing the Mind**: This is the central aspect of reformation. It consists in changing the way we think and perceive the world around us. By immersing ourselves in God's Word, we allow His truth to reshape our understanding and guide our decisions.

2. **Aligning with Scripture**: Reformation calls us to align every aspect of our lives with the teachings of Scripture. This means eval-

uating our beliefs, values, and behaviors in light of God's Word and making necessary changes to reflect His truth.

3. Obedience to God's Commands: A reformed life is characterized by obedience to God. As we grow in our understanding of His will, we must commit to following His commands and living in a way that honors Him.

Revival

Revival, on the other hand, is the outpouring of God's Spirit that brings renewed passion, enthusiasm, and spiritual vitality. It awakens hearts and inspires believers to pursue God with zeal and devotion.

In the Psalms, we find the plea for revival: "Will you not revive us again, that your people may rejoice in you?" (**Psalm 85:6**). Revival is characterized by a renewed sense of God's presence and a deep desire to live out our faith actively and joyfully.

Characteristics of Revival

Revival involves several key characteristics:

1. Renewed Passion for God: Revival ignites a deep and abiding love for God. It stirs our hearts to seek Him with renewed fervor and devotion.

2. Increased Spiritual Awareness: During revival, believers experience a heightened awareness of God's presence and a desire to draw closer to Him.

3. Transformation of Lives: Revival leads to lasting change in the lives of individuals and communities. It inspires believers to live out their faith with authenticity and purpose.

The Relationship Between Reformation and Revival

The relationship between reformation and revival is symbiotic. Reformation prepares us to receive revival by reshaping our minds and hearts to be receptive to God's Spirit. In turn, revival deepens and enhances the changes initiated by reformation, leading to more incredible spiritual growth and impact.

As Jesus explained in **Luke 5:37-38**, "And no one pours new wine into old wineskins. Otherwise, the new wine will burst the skins, the wine will run out, and the wineskins will be ruined. No, new wine must be poured into new wineskins."

This teaching underscores the importance of having a reformed mind—a new wineskin—to hold and sustain the new wine of revival. Without reformation, revival can be short-lived, as the renewed mind provides the structure and understanding needed to maintain and grow in the spiritual renewal God brings.

How Reformation and Revival Work Together

1. **Reformation Prepares the Heart**: By renewing our minds and aligning our lives with God's Word, we create a fertile ground for revival to take root. A reformed heart is ready to receive the outpouring of God's Spirit.

2. **Revival Strengthens Reformation**: Revival deepens the changes initiated by reformation, infusing our faith with new life and vitality. It inspires us to pursue God with greater zeal and devotion.

3. **Sustaining Long-Term Transformation**: Together, reformation and revival lead to lasting change. As we experience revival, the foundation of reformation ensures that the spiritual renewal is sustained over time.

Application

Reflect on the areas of your life that need reformation. How can you renew your mind to align more closely with God's Word? Consider the changes you need to make to create a new wineskin capable of sustaining revival.

1. **Renew Your Mind**: Spend time in God's Word, allowing His truth to reshape your thinking and guide your decisions. Reflect on how you can align your beliefs, values, and behaviors with Scripture.

2. **Pray for Revival**: Ask God to bring revival into your heart and community. Pray for a renewed passion for Him and a desire to live out your faith actively and joyfully.

3. **Embrace Change**: Be open to the changes that reformation and revival bring. Allow God to transform you from the inside out, equipping you to live out your faith powerfully and authentically.

Challenge Questions

1. What areas of your life require reformation, and how can you actively work to renew your mind? Reflect on the changes you need to make to align your life more closely with God's Word.

2. How can you prepare your heart and mind to receive and sustain revival in your life and community? Consider the steps you can take to cultivate a receptive heart and spirit.

3. Reflect on a time when you experienced a revival in your life. How did it impact your faith, and what steps can you take to ensure that revival continues to grow? Reflect on the lessons you learned during that time and how you can apply them to your current circumstances.

By embracing both reformation and revival, we allow God to transform us from the inside out, equipping us to live out our faith powerfully and authentically. As we commit to this journey, may we find strength and encouragement in the knowledge that we are fulfilling God's calling and making a difference in the lives of others?

Day 7:

God Can Use You!

Throughout history, God has chosen to work through imperfect and broken people to accomplish His divine purposes. The Bible is filled with stories of individuals who, by worldly standards, were not qualified to be used by God. Yet, God called them, empowered them, and used them to do incredible things for His glory. This truth is a powerful reminder that no matter our past or perceived shortcomings, God can use us to make a difference in the world.

Biblical Examples of Imperfection

The Bible provides numerous examples of individuals who seemed unfit for God's work. Despite their weaknesses and failures, God used them mightily. Here are a few examples:

1. Elijah was Suicidal

Elijah, a mighty prophet, once despaired of life itself. After a great victory against the prophets of Baal, he fled into the wilderness, overwhelmed and wishing to die. But God met Elijah in his darkest moment, providing comfort and guidance for the path ahead.

1 Kings 19:4 tells us, "He came to a broom bush, sat down under it, and prayed that he might die. 'I have had enough, Lord,' he said. 'Take my life; I am no better than my ancestors.'"

Despite his despair, God restored Elijah and continued to use him as a powerful voice for His purposes.

2. Joseph was Abused

Joseph endured betrayal and abuse at the hands of his own brothers, being sold into slavery and later imprisoned unjustly. Yet, God had a plan for Joseph's life, using him to save an entire nation from famine and to bring reconciliation to his family.

Genesis 50:20 reveals Joseph's perspective: "You intended to harm me, but God intended it for good to accomplish what is now being done, the saving of many lives."

Through Joseph's trials, God worked to bring about a greater purpose, demonstrating His ability to use even the most painful experiences for His glory.

3. Job was Bankrupt

Job lost everything he had—his wealth, his health, and his family. Despite his intense suffering, Job remained faithful to God, ultimately being restored and blessed beyond measure.

Job 42:10 states, "After Job had prayed for his friends, the Lord restored his fortunes and gave him twice as much as he had before."

Job's story reminds us that God can use even our most profound losses to bring about more incredible blessings and insights into His character.

4. Gideon was Afraid

Gideon was called by God to deliver Israel from the oppression of the Midianites, yet he initially doubted his ability to fulfill this calling. Despite his fear, God assured Gideon of His presence and empowered him to lead a victorious battle.

Judges 6:15 records Gideon's response: "Pardon me, my lord," Gideon replied, "but how can I save Israel? My clan is the weakest in Manasseh, and I am the least in my family."

God's response demonstrates that His power is made perfect in our weakness, and He can use us despite our fears.

5. Samson was a Womanizer

Samson, known for his great strength, struggled with personal weaknesses, particularly in his relationships. Yet, even in his failures, God used Samson to deliver Israel from their enemies.

Judges 16:28 captures Samson's final prayer: "Then Samson prayed to the Lord, 'Sovereign Lord, remember me. Please, God, strengthen me just once more, and let me with one blow get revenge on the Philistines for my two eyes.'"

In his final moments, Samson fulfilled his calling and demonstrated that God can use us despite our past mistakes.

6. Paul was a Mass Murderer

Before his conversion, Paul (formerly Saul) persecuted the early Christians, approving of their imprisonment and death. Yet, after encountering Jesus on the road to Damascus, Paul became one of the most influential apostles in spreading the Gospel.

Acts 9:15 records God's words to Ananias: "Go! This man is my chosen instrument to proclaim my name to the Gentiles and their kings and to the people of Israel."

Paul's transformation is a testament to God's grace and His ability to use anyone for His purposes.

7. Moses had a Speech Problem.

Moses, called to lead the Israelites out of Egypt, doubted his ability to speak effectively. Yet, God assured Moses of His presence and provided Aaron as a spokesperson.

Exodus 4:10 recounts Moses' hesitation: "Moses said to the Lord, 'Pardon your servant, Lord. I have never been eloquent, neither in the past nor since you have spoken to your servant. I am slow of speech and tongue.'"

Despite his limitations, Moses became a great leader and prophet, demonstrating that God's strength is sufficient in our weaknesses.

8. Rahab was a Prostitute

Rahab, a woman with a sinful past, played a crucial role in the Israelite conquest of Jericho by hiding the spies. Her faith and courage led to her inclusion in the lineage of Jesus Christ.

Hebrews 11:31 commends her faith: "By faith the prostitute Rahab, because she welcomed the spies, was not killed with those who were disobedient."

Rahab's story shows that God's grace extends to all, regardless of their past, and He can use anyone willing to trust Him.

9. David was a Murderer

David, known as a man after God's own heart, committed adultery and orchestrated the murder of Uriah. Yet, after repenting, David was restored and continued to lead Israel.

Psalm 51:10 reflects David's repentance: "Create in me a pure heart, O God, and renew a steadfast spirit within me."

David's life demonstrates that God's mercy is abundant, and He can use us despite our failures.

10. Jonah was a Coward

Jonah initially ran from God's call to preach to Nineveh, fearing the task before him. Yet, after being swallowed by a great fish and redirected by God, Jonah fulfilled his mission, leading to the repentance of an entire city.

Jonah 3:1-2 records God's command: "Then the word of the Lord came to Jonah a second time: 'Go to the great city of Nineveh and proclaim to it the message I give you.'"

Jonah's story shows that God can use us even when we are reluctant, and His purposes will prevail.

11. Noah was a Drunk

Noah, who faithfully built the ark and preserved humanity, struggled with drunkenness after the flood. Yet, God used Noah to start a new beginning for creation.

Genesis 9:20-21 recounts Noah's actions: "Noah, a man of the soil, proceeded to plant a vineyard. When he drank some of its wine, he became drunk and lay uncovered inside his tent."

Despite his shortcomings, Noah's obedience saved humanity, showing that God can use imperfect people for His plans.

12. Peter was a Liar

Peter, one of Jesus' closest disciples, denied knowing Him three times out of fear. Yet, after Jesus' resurrection, Peter became a bold leader in the early church.

Matthew 26:75 captures Peter's remorse: "Then Peter remembered the word Jesus had spoken: 'Before the rooster crows, you will disown me three times.' And he went outside and wept bitterly."

Peter's transformation illustrates that God's forgiveness is available, and He can use us even after our failures.

God Specializes in Using Broken People

Still think you're too messed up for God to use you? God specializes in using broken people to do powerful things. Are you flawed? **Good.** God can use you! The stories of these biblical figures remind us that our weaknesses and failures do not disqualify us from God's service. Instead, they position us to rely on His strength and grace.

Application

Reflect on your own life and consider the areas where you feel inadequate or unqualified. How might God be calling you to serve despite these perceived limitations? Trust that God can use you, just as He used these individuals, to fulfill His purposes.

1. **Acknowledge Your Weaknesses**: Recognize that everyone has weaknesses and past failures. Bring them before God and ask for His forgiveness and guidance.

2. **Trust in God's Grace**: Remember that God's grace is sufficient for you, and He can use you despite your imperfections. Trust in His power to transform and work through you.

3. **Embrace God's Call**: Be open to the ways God may be calling you to serve. Step out in faith, knowing that He equips those He calls and provides the strength needed to fulfill His purposes.

Challenge Questions

1. What areas of your life make you feel unqualified for God's work? Reflect on how God used the people in the Bible despite their weaknesses and how He can use you.

2. How can you embrace God's grace and allow Him to work through your imperfections? Consider the ways you can trust in His power and surrender your limitations to Him.

3. In what ways can you step out in faith and serve God, trusting that He will equip and empower you? Reflect on the opportunities God has placed before you and how you can respond to His call.

By acknowledging our weaknesses and trusting in God's grace, we position ourselves to be used by Him in powerful ways. As we embrace our identity as vessels of His love and truth, we can impact the world for His glory, demonstrating that God, indeed, can use anyone for His purpose.

Day 8:

When God Drags Us – Helko

One of the profound truths of the Christian faith is the recognition that we cannot come to Jesus on our own. In **John 6:44**, Jesus states, *"No one can come to me unless the Father who sent me draws them."* The Greek word translated as "draw" in this verse is **helko**, which means "to drag." This implies a forceful, compelling action that brings us to Jesus despite our resistance or reluctance.

The Need to Be Dragged

Our human nature, often referred to as the flesh, naturally resists God. Our desires, fears, and misconceptions can keep us from fully embracing the goodness that God offers. The notion of being "dragged" reflects the reality that, left to our own devices, we might never choose to seek God or recognize our need for Him.

The apostle Paul describes this struggle in **Romans 7:18-19**: *"For I know that good itself does not dwell in me, that is, in my sinful nature. For I have the desire to do what is good, but I cannot carry it out. For I do not do the good I want to do, but the evil I do not want to do—this I keep on doing."*

Paul's words resonate with the human experience of wrestling with sin and the inability to align our actions with our desires for goodness. This internal conflict highlights the necessity of God's intervention.

God's Grace in Dragging Us

God's intervention is necessary to overcome our resistance and lead us to a relationship with Him. The act of being dragged is an expression of God's grace, showing that He actively seeks us out, even when we are lost in our own ways. It is a reminder that God's love is relentless and that He pursues us with a fervor that transcends our reluctance.

Accepting the Kingdom

While God drags us toward Him, we still need to make a conscious decision to accept His Kingdom. God's compelling draw is an invitation to open our hearts and minds to His truth and love. Our response requires humility, surrender, and a willingness to let go of our preconceived notions and fears.

In **John 6:65**, Jesus reinforces this idea: *"This is why I told you that no one can come to me unless the Father has enabled them."* God enables us, but we must choose to embrace that enablement and walk in His ways.

The Role of Free Will

Though God's draw is mighty, He respects our free will. We must choose to respond to His call, to say "yes" to His invitation, and to pursue a relationship with Him. This choice is a daily commitment to follow Christ, to seek His will, and to align our lives with His purposes.

The Role of Leaders and Mentors

In a similar way, leaders, mentors, and spiritual fathers play a vital role in guiding others toward spiritual growth and maturity. They often need to "drag" their disciples, encouraging them to engage with teachings they might initially resist or not fully understand. This dragging is not about coercion but about persistent encouragement and guidance, helping others see the value and truth in the teachings of Jesus.

Paul's Example with Timothy

The apostle Paul exemplifies this in his relationship with Timothy. He consistently encourages and instructs Timothy to remain steadfast and to grow in faith and knowledge.

2 Timothy 1:13-14 says, *"What you heard from me, keep as the pattern of sound teaching, with faith and love in Christ Jesus. Guard the good deposit that was entrusted to you—guard it with the help of the Holy Spirit who lives in us."*

Paul's mentorship of Timothy highlights the importance of nurturing spiritual growth through guidance, support, and encouragement.

Mentorship in Our Lives

We, too, need mentors and spiritual leaders who can guide us, challenge us, and support us as we grow in our faith. These relationships provide accountability and encouragement, helping us to stay on course and to persevere through challenges.

Application

Reflect on areas in your life where God might be dragging you toward growth or change. Are there teachings or opportunities that you resist but know deep down are for your good? Consider how you can be more open to God's leading and the guidance of spiritual mentors.

1. **Identify Resistance**: Take time to identify areas where you may be resisting God's call or the guidance of spiritual mentors. Acknowledge the fears or misconceptions that may be holding you back.

2. **Embrace God's Call**: Make a conscious decision to embrace God's call and to be open to His leading. Pray for the willingness to surrender your resistance and to trust in His plans for your life.

3. **Seek Mentorship**: Reach out to spiritual leaders or mentors who can provide guidance and support. Be open to their wisdom and encouragement as you navigate your spiritual journey.

Challenge Questions

1. **In what areas of your life have you felt God dragging you toward a deeper relationship with Him?** Reflect on how you can respond to His call and embrace His invitation to grow.

2. **How can you be more receptive to God's drawing and the guidance of those who mentor you?** Consider the steps you can take to open your heart and mind to their influence.

3. **Reflect on a time when you resisted spiritual growth but later recognized the value of being led by God. How can you apply that lesson now?** Reflect on how you can use past experiences to inform your current spiritual journey.

By allowing God to draw us and embracing the guidance of spiritual leaders, we can experience the fullness of His Kingdom and grow into mature disciples of Christ. As we yield to His leading, may we find strength and encouragement in His presence, trusting that He will guide us every step of the way.

Day 9:

The Cost of the Calling

In our pursuit of purpose and impact, it's natural to focus on achievements and successes. However, in the Kingdom of God, credibility and effectiveness are often forged in the fires of suffering. The more honest and vulnerable we are about our struggles, the more powerful our influence can be in the lives of others. The Apostle Paul is a profound example of how suffering and calling are intertwined.

Paul's Example

When God called Paul, He made it clear that Paul's journey would not be easy. In **Acts 9:15-16**, the Lord tells Ananias, "Go! This man is my chosen instrument to carry my name before the Gentiles and their kings and before the people of Israel. I will show him how much he must suffer for my name."

While we often celebrate Paul's remarkable accomplishments—writing two-thirds of the New Testament, spreading the gospel across the known world, and becoming one of history's greatest missionaries and preachers—we sometimes overlook the suffering that accompanied his calling. Paul's accomplishments and his suffering were not separate but intrinsically connected.

The Suffering of Paul

Paul's life was marked by significant hardships, including imprisonment, beatings, shipwrecks, and constant threats to his life. Despite these challenges, Paul remained steadfast in his mission to spread the Gospel, demonstrating unwavering faith and resilience.

2 Corinthians 11:23-28 provides a glimpse into Paul's suffering: "I have worked much harder, been in prison more frequently, been flogged more severely, and been exposed to death again and again. Five times, I received from the Jews the forty lashes minus one. Three times I was beaten with rods, once I was pelted with stones, three times I was shipwrecked, I spent a night and a day in the open sea, I have been constantly on the move."

Paul's perseverance in the face of such adversity highlights the profound connection between suffering and calling.

The Connection Between Suffering and Calling

Paul's story reveals a crucial truth: in order for him to be significantly used, he had to be wounded deeply. The greater the calling, the greater the cost. God's purpose for Paul included not only outstanding achievements but also significant suffering. This was not because God had a vendetta against Paul, nor was it divine retribution for his past as a persecutor of Christians.

Instead, Paul's suffering was part of God's plan to make him an effective instrument for the Gospel. Through suffering, Paul learned complete reliance on God, developed empathy for those he ministered to, and became a living testimony to God's power in weakness.

God's Purpose in Suffering

Paul's suffering was not without purpose. It refined his character, deepened his faith, and enabled him to empathize with others who faced similar trials. Through his letters, Paul encouraged believers to persevere in the face of adversity, trusting that God was using their trials for a greater purpose.

2 Corinthians 12:9 highlights God's assurance to Paul: "But he said to me, 'My grace is sufficient for you, for my power is made perfect in weakness.' Therefore, I will boast all the more gladly about my weaknesses so that Christ's power may rest on me."

Paul's testimony illustrates that God's power is often revealed most clearly in our moments of weakness.

Embracing the Cost

We often desire to do great things for God without enduring the hardships that come with such a calling. However, as Paul's life shows, God uses our wounds to shape us and to make us more sensitive to His touch. When we experience pain and trials, we are given opportunities to let the light of Christ shine through us, even when everything around us seems dark.

Paul eloquently captures this reality in his letters:

2 Corinthians 4:11 states, "For we who are alive are always being given over to death for Jesus' sake, so that his life may be revealed in our mortal body."

2 Corinthians 4:17 adds, "For our light and momentary troubles are achieving for us an eternal glory that far outweighs them all."

In **Philippians 3:10**, Paul expresses his desire to "know Christ—yes, to know the power of his resurrection and participation in his sufferings, becoming like him in his death."

The Call to Surrender

To embrace the cost of our calling, we must be willing to surrender our desires and expectations, trusting that God's plan is more significant than our own. This surrender requires faith, courage, and a willingness to endure trials for the sake of Christ.

Application

If you genuinely want to be significantly used by God, recognize that it will come at a cost. You may face exhaustion, betrayal, and suffering, but these experiences can deepen your relationship with God and enhance your ministry.

1. **Acknowledge the Cost**: Recognize that the call to follow Christ involves sacrifice and hardship. Be prepared to endure challenges for the sake of the Gospel.

2. **Trust in God's Purpose**: Trust that God is using your suffering to refine you and to make you a more effective witness for His Kingdom. Lean on His strength and guidance in times of difficulty.

3. **Embrace Vulnerability**: Be open about your struggles and weaknesses, allowing others to see God's power at work in your life. Your vulnerability can be a source of encouragement and inspiration to others.

4. **Seek God's Presence**: In moments of suffering, draw near to God in prayer and worship. Allow His presence to comfort and sustain you, knowing that He is with you in every trial.

Challenge Questions

1. **How can you embrace the cost of your calling and trust God to use your suffering for His glory?** Reflect on the ways you can surrender to God's plan and trust in His purpose.

2. **In what ways can you become more vulnerable and honest about your struggles to impact others?** Consider how your testimony can encourage and inspire those around you.

3. **Reflect on a time when God used your pain to shape you or to help others. How can you build on that experience to serve Him more effectively?** Reflect on the lessons you learned and how you can apply them to your current ministry.

By accepting the cost of the calling, you open yourself to being a powerful instrument in God's hands, allowing His strength to be perfected in your weakness. As you navigate the challenges of life, may you find comfort in the knowledge that God is with you, using every experience for His glory and your growth.

Day 10:

The Five Costs of a Leader

Leadership is a calling that comes with significant responsibilities and sacrifices. In **Luke 14:28-30**, Jesus highlights the importance of counting the cost before embarking on any venture:

"For which of you, desiring to build a tower, does not first sit down and count the cost, whether he has enough to complete it? Otherwise, when he has laid a foundation and is not able to finish, all who see it begin to mock him, saying, 'This man began to build and was not able to finish.'"

Effective leadership requires understanding and embracing these costs. Here are five areas where leaders must be willing to pay the price:

1. Financial Cost

Investing in leadership development often comes with a financial price. Whether it's purchasing books, attending conferences, or participating in training programs, personal growth as a leader requires financial investment. Leaders who excel are those who are willing to spend money to stretch themselves and enhance their skills. This willingness reflects a commitment to personal and professional development, recognizing that growth is essential to effective leadership.

Proverbs 4:7 reminds us, *"The beginning of wisdom is this: Get wisdom. Though it cost all you have, get understanding."*

This verse emphasizes the value of wisdom and understanding, which are crucial for effective leadership. Investing in resources that foster growth and learning is a necessary cost that yields long-term benefits.

2. Emotional Cost

Leading in any capacity, especially within the church, can be emotionally draining. Leaders often experience a rollercoaster of emotions, moving from moments of triumph to challenges in an instant. Your heart and motives may be questioned, and you might face criticism from those who do not understand your vision. Emotional resilience is crucial. It requires vulnerability and courage to navigate these highs and lows while remaining steadfast in your calling.

Psalm 34:17-18 offers comfort: *"The righteous cry out, and the Lord hears them; he delivers them from all their troubles. The Lord is close to the brokenhearted and saves those who are crushed in spirit."*

God promises to be near in times of emotional struggle, offering strength and support to leaders as they face challenges. This assurance enables leaders to persevere through emotional costs.

3. Physical Cost

Leadership demands physical energy and stamina. Laziness and leadership do not go hand in hand. Authentic leadership involves hard work, dedication, and perseverance. It requires getting out of bed early, putting in the effort, and maintaining focus, even during demanding seasons. While rest is essential to avoid burnout, leaders must also be willing to invest the necessary time and energy to achieve their goals and support their teams.

1 Corinthians 9:24-27 illustrates the discipline required: *"Do you not know that in a race all the runners run, but only one gets the prize? Run in such a way as to get the prize. Everyone who competes in the games goes into strict training."*

This passage highlights the need for discipline and dedication in leadership, likening it to an athlete's rigorous training. Leaders must be prepared to expend physical effort to fulfill their responsibilities effectively.

4. Spiritual Cost

As leaders grow in influence, they will inevitably face more significant spiritual challenges. Spiritual warfare and temptation are part of the journey, and leaders must be prepared to fight these battles. Maintaining a solid relationship with God is vital. It involves regular prayer, studying the Word, and relying on the Holy Spirit for guidance and strength. Leaders need to remain vigilant, understanding that their spiritual health directly impacts their effectiveness.

Ephesians 6:10-11 encourages leaders: "Finally, be strong in the Lord and in his mighty power. Put on the full armor of God so that you can take your stand against the devil's schemes."

This passage underscores the importance of spiritual preparedness and reliance on God's strength to navigate the challenges of leadership.

5.   **Personal Cost**

All these aspects culminate in a personal cost that affects every leader. Leadership can profoundly impact one's personal life, relationships, and well-being. Jesus exemplified this when He surrendered to the Father's will, fully aware of the individual cost involved in going to the cross. Yet, He embraced His mission with joy, knowing the eternal significance of His sacrifice.

Philippians 2:5-8 highlights Jesus' example: *"In your relationships with one another, have the same mindset as Christ Jesus: Who, being in very nature God, did not consider equality with God something to be used to his own advantage; rather, he made himself nothing by taking the very nature of a servant, being made in human likeness. And being found in appearance as a man, he humbled himself by becoming obedient to death—even death on a cross!"*

Jesus' sacrifice exemplifies the ultimate personal cost of leadership, serving as a model for leaders to follow with humility and dedication.

Galatians 6:9 encourages us: *"And let us not grow weary of doing good, for in due season we will reap if we do not give up."*

This promise should resonate with every leader. The price of leadership is high, but the rewards are eternal. As leaders, we must remain focused on our calling, trusting that God will sustain us through the challenges.

Challenge Questions

1. Which of the five costs resonates most with you, and how can you prepare to pay that price in your leadership journey? Reflect on your personal leadership journey and identify areas where you can invest more effort or resources.

2. How can you balance the demands of leadership with your personal well-being and spiritual health? Consider strategies for maintaining a healthy balance, such as prioritizing self-care and seeking support from mentors and peers.

3. Reflect on a time when you experienced one of these costs. How did it shape your growth as a leader, and what lessons can you apply moving forward? Reflect on past experiences and use them as learning opportunities to enhance your leadership skills.

Remember, the ultimate example of sacrificial leadership is Jesus, whose assignment was far more demanding than ours. His joy in fulfilling His mission should inspire us to persevere and not give up. Embrace the costs, for they are the path to meaningful and impactful leadership.

Day 11:

A Study on Focus

In the fast-paced world we live in, maintaining focus can be challenging. Yet, focus is essential for productivity and spiritual growth. It allows us to concentrate on what truly matters and to align our lives with our goals and values. The Bible encourages us to fix our eyes on Jesus, the ultimate example of focus and perseverance.

Biblical Perspective

Hebrews 12:2 (NIV) states, "Fixing our eyes on Jesus, the pioneer and perfecter of faith. For the joy set before him, he endured the cross, scorning its shame, and sat down at the right hand of the throne of God."

This verse calls us to center our focus on Jesus, who remained steadfast in His mission despite immense suffering. His focus on the joy set before Him empowered Him to endure the cross and complete His work of salvation. By looking to Jesus, we learn to maintain focus on our spiritual goals despite distractions and challenges.

The Importance of Focus

Focus is not easy to achieve, but it is necessary for living a purposeful life. Anyone can exist and survive without much effort, but realizing productivity and fulfillment requires intentional focus.

To focus is to have vision. It means aligning your thoughts and actions with your goals. Focus involves:

- **Convergence**: Coming into unity with yourself, others, and God. It requires harmony between your values and actions.

- **Concentration**: Directing your attention toward what matters most. This involves prioritizing tasks and eliminating distractions.

- **Meditation**: Reflecting on God's Word and His purposes for your life. Regular meditation keeps your spiritual compass aligned.

- **Unity**: Joining together in a shared vision and mission. Working with others amplifies your focus and effectiveness.

Focus must be both personal and corporate, involving commitment to God and to serving others. It requires submitting to God's authority and aligning our lives with His will. Proper focus transforms not just individual lives but entire communities, fostering a shared sense of purpose and direction.

The Illusion of Focus

However, focus has an illusion known as the "Focusing Illusion." This phenomenon occurs when our perception is distorted by misplaced focus.

The Mall Effect

A trip to the mall can shift our focus from gratitude to greed. Malls are designed to make us focus on what we lack, breeding discontent and desire for more. This can lead to unnecessary spending and a constant feeling of inadequacy.

To counteract this, experiencing life in a developing country can help us appreciate what we have, highlighting the stark contrast between our abundance and others' lack.

The Mission Trip Effect

Seeing what others do not have fosters gratitude and contentment. It shifts our focus from wanting more to appreciating the blessings we already possess. This perspective change helps cultivate a heart of thankfulness and generosity, allowing us to find joy in simplicity and sufficiency.

A Study on College Students

A study involving college students illustrated the focusing illusion. When asked, "How happy are you?" and "How many dates have you had in the last month?" the order of the questions affected their perceived happiness. Focusing on their dating status caused students to feel less happy, emphasizing how focus can distort reality.

This study demonstrates that what we choose to focus on directly impacts our emotions and perceptions. By consciously directing our focus, we can shape a more positive and fulfilling reality.

Shifting Your Focus

Our focus determines our reality. The questions we ask ourselves and the perspectives we adopt shape our lives:

- **Financial Focus**: Are you focused on what you have or what you don't have? This distinction defines gratitude versus greed. When we focus on abundance, we cultivate contentment and generosity.

- **Eternal Focus**: Are you focused on this life or the next? This distinction defines stinginess versus generosity. Focusing on eternity helps prioritize lasting values over temporary gains.

- **Relational Focus**: Are you focused on your wants or others' needs? This distinction defines selfishness versus compassion and influences our joy and contentment. Serving others can lead to more profound satisfaction and a sense of purpose.

As our focus changes, our perspective changes, and ultimately, our lives change. By fixing our eyes on Jesus and maintaining a focus grounded in faith and gratitude, we align our lives with God's purposes and experience true fulfillment.

Philippians 4:8 encourages us to focus on positive and noble things: "Finally, brothers and sisters, whatever is true, whatever is noble, whatever is right, whatever is pure, whatever is lovely, whatever is admirable—if anything is excellent or praiseworthy—think about such things."

Application

To cultivate focus, begin by identifying areas where distraction and misplaced priorities creep in. Set aside regular time for prayer and reflection to align your focus with God's will. Surround yourself with others who share your values and can support you in maintaining your focus.

1. **Identify Distractions**: Reflect on what distracts you from focusing on your goals and values. Consider how you can eliminate or minimize these distractions to maintain clarity.

2. **Prioritize Prayer and Reflection**: Make time for prayer and meditation, seeking God's guidance and wisdom. This practice helps

realign your focus with His purposes and strengthens your spiritual foundation.

3.   Seek Support: Build a community of like-minded individuals who can encourage and challenge you to stay focused. Surrounding yourself with people who share your values helps reinforce your commitment to living a purposeful life.

Challenge Questions

1. How can you align your focus with God's purposes, ensuring that your life reflects His values and priorities?
Reflect on your current focus and consider how you can shift it to align with God's will.

2. In what areas of your life do you need to shift your focus from what you lack to appreciating what you have?
Practice gratitude by recognizing and celebrating the blessings in your life.

3. How can you cultivate a focus that emphasizes others' needs over your own desires, fostering compassion and joy?
Look for opportunities to serve others and make a positive impact in their lives.

Remember, your focus determines your reality. By choosing to focus on Jesus and His example, you can navigate life with clarity, purpose, and joy. Embrace focus as a tool for spiritual growth and productivity, and watch as your life becomes a testament to God's transformative power.

Day 12:

What God Uses to Form Us

Life's challenges and trials are often the very tools God uses to mold us into the people He desires us to be. Our natural instincts may lead us to avoid discomfort, seek approval, and crave control. Yet, it is precisely through experiences of rejection, humiliation, suffering, and uncertainty that God forms our character and strengthens our faith.

The Role of Trials in Spiritual Formation

The Bible teaches that trials and difficulties are not meaningless; they are purposeful in God's plan for our growth. Trials serve as catalysts for spiritual development, pushing us beyond our comfort zones and forcing us to rely on God's strength and wisdom.

James 1:2-4 (NIV) states, "Consider it pure joy, my brothers and sisters, whenever you face trials of many kinds because you know that the testing of your faith produces perseverance. Let perseverance finish its work so that you may be mature and complete, not lacking anything."

This passage encourages us to view challenges as opportunities for growth. By embracing trials, we open ourselves to God's transformative work in our lives, developing resilience and maturity. Trials are not merely obstacles to be overcome but are essential elements of our spiritual journey, shaping us into the image of Christ.

God Uses Rejection to Shape Us

For the approval addict, rejection is the greatest fear. The desire for acceptance and validation from others can be overwhelming. However, God uses rejection to redirect our focus to Him. Rejection strips away the illusion that our worth is tied to human approval and reminds us of our true identity in Christ.

Psalm 118:8-9 reminds us, "It is better to take refuge in the Lord than to trust in humans. It is better to take refuge in the Lord than to trust in princes."

Rejection teaches us that our worth and identity are found in God, not in the opinions of others. By experiencing rejection, we learn to rely on God's acceptance and love, which are unwavering and unconditional. This shift in perspective helps us find security and confidence in our relationship with God, freeing us from the chains of people-pleasing.

God Uses Humiliation to Humble Us

For those addicted to power, the fear of humiliation can be paralyzing. Yet, God uses these moments to humble us and remind us of our dependence on Him. Humiliation breaks down our pride, teaching us to see ourselves and others through God's eyes.

Philippians 2:3-4 encourages us, "Do nothing out of selfish ambition or vain conceit. Rather, in humility, value others above yourselves, not looking to your own interests but each of you to the interests of the others."

Through humiliation, we learn to let go of pride and ego, developing a servant-hearted attitude that mirrors Christ's humility. Humiliation teaches us to see others as valuable and to place their needs above our own. This transformation enables us to serve selflessly and to build authentic, loving relationships.

God Uses Suffering to Strengthen Us

The comfort addict dreads suffering, seeking to avoid pain at all costs. Yet, suffering is often where we experience God's presence most profoundly. In the midst of our pain, we encounter God's comfort, grace, and strength.

Romans 5:3-5 tells us, "Not only so, but we also glory in our sufferings, because we know that suffering produces perseverance; perseverance, character; and character, hope. And hope does not put us to shame because God's love has been poured out into our hearts through the Holy Spirit, who has been given to us."

Suffering refines us, stripping away superficialities and drawing us closer to God. In our pain, we find strength and hope through His love and grace. Suffering becomes a means of deepening our faith and trust in God, teaching us to rely on Him in all circumstances.

God Uses Uncertainty to Build Trust

For the control addict, uncertainty is a source of anxiety. The desire to predict and manage every aspect of life can lead to frustration. Yet, God uses uncertainty to teach us to trust Him fully. Uncertainty forces us to surrender our plans and to lean on God's wisdom and timing.

Proverbs 3:5-6 instructs us, "Trust in the Lord with all your heart and lean not on your own understanding; in all your ways submit to him, and he will make your paths straight."

Uncertainty forces us to let go of our illusion of control and to place our faith in God's perfect plan. In doing so, we learn to rely on His wisdom and guidance, which are far greater than our own. This reliance on God leads to peace and confidence, knowing that He is sovereign over every detail of our lives.

Application

Reflect on the areas in your life where God may be using trials to shape you. Are you facing rejection, humiliation, suffering, or uncertainty? Instead of resisting these experiences, embrace them as opportunities for growth. Ask God to reveal the lessons He wants to teach you through these challenges and to give you the strength to persevere.

1. **Embrace Trials as Growth Opportunities**: Recognize that challenges are part of God's plan for your spiritual development. Rather than avoiding them, seek to understand how God is using them to refine your character and deepen your faith.

2. **Trust in God's Sovereignty**: Trust that God is in control, even when circumstances are complex or uncertain. Surrender your fears and anxieties to Him, knowing that He is working all things together for your good.

3. **Seek God's Presence**: In moments of suffering or humiliation, draw near to God in prayer and worship. Allow His presence to comfort and sustain you, knowing that He is with you in every trial.

Challenge Questions

1. How can you reframe your perspective on trials, viewing them as opportunities for growth rather than obstacles? Consider how you can shift your mindset to embrace challenges as part of God's transformative work in your life.

2. In what ways can you learn to trust God more fully in areas where you seek approval, power, comfort, or control? Reflect on the places where you struggle with trust and strive to surrender those areas to God.

3. Reflect on a past experience where God used a difficult situation to form your character. How can you apply that lesson to your current circumstances? Consider how you can build on past experiences to navigate current challenges with faith and resilience.

By allowing God to use life's challenges to form us, we become more like Christ, embodying His love, humility, and strength. Embrace the process, trusting that God is working all things together for your good and His glory. As you navigate the trials of life, may you find peace and joy in knowing that God is shaping you into the person He created you to be.

Day 13:

The Secret to Revelation

In our journey of faith, we often seek more profound understanding and revelation from God. However, the path to revelation is not through intellectual pursuit alone but through embracing mystery and childlikeness. The level of revelation God gives us is often equal to the level of mystery we are willing to live with. This willingness to embrace mystery is rooted in our capacity to remain childlike in our faith.

Embracing Mystery

Mystery is an inherent part of our relationship with God. As finite beings, we cannot fully comprehend the infinite nature of God. His ways and thoughts are higher than ours.

Isaiah 55:8-9 (NIV) declares, "For my thoughts are not your thoughts, neither are your ways my ways," declares the Lord. "As the heavens are higher than the earth, so are my ways higher than your ways and my thoughts than your thoughts."

Embracing mystery means accepting that we will not always have clear answers or complete understanding. It requires humility and trust, recognizing that God's wisdom surpasses our own. This acceptance allows us to rest in the assurance that God is sovereign and His plans are perfect, even when they are beyond our comprehension.

Jesus' Use of Parables

Jesus often spoke in parables, leaving listeners with truths that required reflection and contemplation. He invited them to seek deeper meaning rather than offering straightforward explanations. This approach encouraged people to embrace the mystery and engage with the truths of the Kingdom on a deeper level.

Matthew 13:10-11 (NIV) explains, "The disciples came to him and asked, 'Why do you speak to the people in parables?' He replied, 'Because the knowledge of the secrets of the kingdom of heaven has been given to you, but not to them.'"

Through parables, Jesus revealed that understanding the mysteries of the Kingdom requires a heart open to exploration and discovery.

The Role of Childlikeness

Childlikeness is not about being childish but about maintaining a posture of humility, wonder, and trust. Children naturally embrace mystery because they live in a world entirely of things they do not yet understand. They trust their caregivers implicitly and are open to learning and experiencing new things.

Jesus emphasized the importance of childlikeness in Matthew 18:3-4 (NIV): "Truly I tell you, unless you change and become like little children, you will never enter the kingdom of heaven. Therefore, whoever takes the lowly position of this child is the greatest in the kingdom of heaven."

Childlikeness allows us to access dimensions and realms of the Kingdom that are otherwise inaccessible. It opens our hearts to receive revelation from God with simplicity and purity. This childlike faith invites us to approach God with a sense of wonder, curiosity, and openness, ready to receive whatever He desires to reveal to us.

Living with Mystery

The inability to live with mystery is often a resistance to childlikeness. As adults, we tend to seek control and certainty, usually struggling with the unknown. However, God invites us to surrender our need for complete understanding and to trust Him fully.

The Apostle Paul's Perspective

Despite his vast knowledge and understanding, the Apostle Paul recognized the importance of mystery.

1 Corinthians 13:12 (NIV) states, "For now we see only a reflection as in a mirror; then we shall see face to face. Now I know in part; then I shall know fully, even as I am fully known."

Living with mystery means accepting that our understanding is partial and trusting that God will reveal what we need to know in His perfect timing. This perspective frees us from the burden of having to know everything and allows us to rest in God's wisdom and guidance.

Trusting God in the Unknown

Trusting God in the unknown requires a shift in focus from our need for answers to our relationship with Him. It involves letting go of our desire for control and embracing the uncertainty of life with confidence in God's goodness and faithfulness.

The Secret to Revelation

The secret to revelation lies in our willingness to embrace mystery and maintain a childlike faith. When we approach God with humility, wonder, and trust, He reveals Himself to us in profound ways. This revelation is not just intellectual but experiential, transforming our hearts and drawing us closer to Him.

Proverbs 25:2 (NIV) says, "It is the glory of God to conceal a matter; to search out a matter is the glory of kings."

God delights in revealing His truths to those who earnestly seek Him, and He often uses mystery as a means to draw us into a deeper relationship with Him. As we embrace the mysteries of God, we open ourselves to the possibility of experiencing His presence and guidance in new and unexpected ways.

Application

Reflect on your current relationship with mystery and childlikeness. Are you willing to embrace the unknown and trust God's wisdom and timing? Consider how you can cultivate a more childlike faith, approaching God with openness and wonder.

    1. **Embrace the Unknown**: Accept that there will always be aspects of God and His plans that remain mysterious. Allow this mystery to deepen your trust and reliance on Him.

    2. **Cultivate Childlikeness**: Approach your faith with a sense of wonder and curiosity, ready to learn and grow. Trust in God's goodness and be open to His leading, even when it doesn't make sense.

    3. **Seek God's Revelation**: Spend time in prayer, asking God to reveal Himself to you in new and profound ways. Be willing to let go of your need for control and certainty, trusting that He will guide you.

Challenge Questions

1. How can you embrace mystery in your spiritual journey, allowing it to deepen your faith and reliance on God? Reflect on the ways you can surrender your need for answers and trust in God's wisdom.

2. In what areas of your life do you struggle with the need for control or certainty, and how can you cultivate a more childlike faith? Consider how you can let go of your desire for power and trust God more fully.

3. Reflect on a time when God revealed something to you in a way that required you to embrace mystery. How did that experience impact your relationship with Him? Think about how you can apply that experience to your current walk with God.

By embracing mystery and cultivating a childlike faith, we open ourselves to the profound revelations God desires to share with us. Trust in His wisdom, and allow the mysteries of His Kingdom to draw you into a deeper relationship with Him. As you journey through life, may you find joy and peace in the knowledge that God is with you, guiding you and revealing His truths in His perfect timing?

Day 14:

Love vs. Tolerance

In today's world, the concepts of love and tolerance are often confused or conflated. While love is a biblical command, tolerance is frequently portrayed as a virtue in our culture. However, the two could not be more different. Understanding this distinction is crucial for anchoring our values in God's Word rather than in a world's broken system.

Biblical Warning Against Tolerance

In the book of Revelation, Jesus warns the church in Thyatira about the dangers of tolerance. **Revelation 2:20 (NIV)** states, "Nevertheless, I have this against you: You tolerate that woman Jezebel, who calls herself a prophet. By her teaching, she misleads my servants into sexual immorality and the eating of food sacrificed to idols."

The church in Thyatira was praised for their love, faith, and service, but they were criticized for tolerating immorality and idolatry. Their failure to address sin and false teaching within the church led to spiritual compromise. This passage highlights that tolerance, when it allows sin to flourish, is not a virtue but a vice that can lead believers away from the truth.

Jesus' message to the church in Thyatira serves as a powerful reminder that we must be vigilant in upholding God's standards. Tolerance that permits sin to persist is not loving; it is harmful. It undermines the truth and weakens the spiritual integrity of individuals and communities.

The Difference Between Love and Tolerance

Understanding the difference between love and tolerance is essential for navigating relationships and conflicts in a way that honors God.

Love Seeks the Other Person's Good

Love, as described in the Bible, is selfless and sacrificial. It seeks the well-being of others, even when it requires difficult conversations or actions. True love aligns with God's commands and aims to guide others toward righteousness and truth.

1 Corinthians 13:6 (NIV) reminds us, "Love does not delight in evil but rejoices with the truth." Genuine love involves guiding others toward God's truth and helping them grow in their faith.

Love is not afraid to address sin because it desires what is best for the other person. It is willing to confront wrongdoing and encourage change, all while demonstrating grace and compassion. Love's goal is to build up and strengthen others, leading them closer to God.

Tolerance Seeks to Be Thought of as Good

In contrast, tolerance often prioritizes avoiding conflict and seeking approval from others. It can lead to condoning behaviors that contradict God's Word. Tolerance, in this sense, can stem from a desire to be liked or accepted rather than a commitment to the truth.

Tolerance may seem like the easier path because it avoids confrontation and maintains a superficial peace. However, when tolerance comes at the expense of truth, it ultimately does a disservice to those we aim to protect. It allows sin to persist unchallenged, preventing real growth and transformation.

Love Comes from Fearing God

Love is rooted in a reverence for God and His commandments. When we love God, we naturally desire to follow His ways and encourage others to do the same. This means addressing sin and guiding others toward repentance and transformation.

Love is grounded in a deep respect for God's holiness and a desire to honor Him in all things. It recognizes that true love cannot exist apart from truth, and it seeks to uphold God's standards in every aspect of life.

Tolerance Comes from Fearing Man

Tolerance, as promoted by the world, can be motivated by a fear of man—a desire to fit in or avoid criticism. This fear can lead to compromising God's standards to maintain peace or acceptance.

Proverbs 29:25 (NIV) warns, "Fear of man will prove to be a snare, but whoever trusts in the Lord is kept safe." Tolerance rooted in fear of man can trap us in a cycle of compromise, hindering our ability to stand firm in God's truth.

Love in Action

Nowhere in Scripture is tolerance held up as a virtue. Instead, we are called to love others as God loves us—truthfully, sacrificially, and unconditionally. Jesus demonstrated this love throughout His ministry. He welcomed sinners, but He never condoned their sin. Instead, He called them to repentance and transformation.

In **John 8:11 (NIV)**, Jesus tells the woman caught in adultery, "Neither do I condemn you; go and sin no more." Jesus showed love by offering forgiveness and urging her to turn away from sin. His approach exemplifies how love, not tolerance, leads to true healing and change.

Jesus' example teaches us that love is not passive but active. It seeks to bring about transformation and growth by addressing sin with grace and truth. Love calls us to engage with others in a way that reflects God's heart and desires for their lives.

Anchoring Our Values in God's Word

As believers, it is essential to anchor our values in God's Word, not in a world's broken system. The world may promote tolerance as a virtue, but Scripture calls us to a higher standard of love—one that seeks the best for others, even when it is uncomfortable.

Romans 12:2 (NIV) urges us, "Do not conform to the pattern of this world, but be transformed by the renewing of your mind." Our minds and hearts must be shaped by God's truth, allowing us to discern the difference between love and tolerance.

By aligning our values with God's Word, we are equipped to navigate the complexities of life with wisdom and discernment. We can stand firm in our convictions and extend genuine love to those around us.

Application

Reflect on your approach to relationships and conflicts. Are you prioritizing tolerance over love? Consider how you can demonstrate true love by speaking the truth in love, holding firm to God's standards, and guiding others toward righteousness.

1. **Evaluate Your Approach**: Take time to assess how you handle difficult conversations and situations. Are you avoiding conflict to maintain peace, or are you addressing issues with love and truth?

2. **Seek God's Wisdom**: Pray for wisdom and courage to address sin and immorality with love and grace. Ask God to help you navigate difficult conversations with compassion and truth, always seeking the good of others and the glory of God.

3. **Commit to Growth**: Commit to growing in your understanding of biblical love and how to apply it in your relationships. Surround yourself with others who share your values and can support you in living out God's truth.

Challenge Questions

1. How can you demonstrate love that seeks the other person's good, even when it requires difficult conversations or actions? Reflect on specific ways you can show love by addressing sin with grace and truth.

2. In what areas of your life have you allowed tolerance to overshadow biblical love? How can you realign your values with God's Word? Consider how you can strengthen your commitment to God's standards and encourage others to do the same.

3. Reflect on a time when you faced pressure to tolerate something that contradicted God's standards. How did you respond, and what did you learn from that experience? Use this reflection to guide your future interactions and decisions.

By choosing love over tolerance, we align our lives with God's truth and become instruments of His grace and transformation in the world. Embrace the challenge of living out genuine love, trusting that God will use it to bring about lasting change and redemption. As we prioritize love, may we reflect the heart of Christ and draw others into a deeper relationship with Him.

Day 15:

Religious Hypocrisy

One of the most damaging aspects of religious life is hypocrisy. We often find ourselves judging others for their sins while overlooking our own shortcomings. This tendency to judge people who sin differently than we do can lead to self-righteousness, division, and a lack of grace within the community of believers. Understanding and addressing religious hypocrisy is essential for fostering genuine relationships and reflecting Christ's love.

Understanding Sin and Hypocrisy

The Bible clearly defines various sins that are prevalent in our culture today. These include:

• **Homosexuality and Transgenderism**: **Romans 1:26-27** and **Romans 1:24** describe these behaviors as contrary to God's design. Teaching children that these practices are natural and good also contradicts biblical teaching (**Matthew 18:6**).

• **Killing Babies**: **Exodus 20:13** commands, "You shall not murder," which applies to all human life, including the unborn.

• **Fornication**: **Ephesians 5:3** warns against sexual immorality, urging believers to maintain purity.

• **Divorce**: While divorce is allowed in certain circumstances, Jesus teaches that it is a sin in most cases (**Matthew 5:31-32**).

• **Dishonesty**: Lying, exaggerations, half-truths, and embellishments are sins (**Colossians 3:9**).

• **Worldliness**: Aligning with worldly values is a sin (**James 4:4**).

• **Neglecting the Needy**: Failing to care for foreigners, the poor, widows, and the fatherless is a sin (**Leviticus 19:33-34**, **1 John 3:17-18**, **Exodus 22:22-23**).

- **Favoritism**: Treating people of influence with more honor than those without is a sin (**James 2:1**).

- **False Prophecy**: Speaking the dictates of your own heart as the Word of God is sin (**Jeremiah 14:14**).

- **Slander**: Speaking ill of others is sin (**James 4:11**).

- **Pride**: **Proverbs 16:5** warns that pride is detestable to God.

- **Unbelief**: Not believing in who Jesus says He is a sin (**John 6:64**).

- **Unforgiveness**: Failing to forgive others is a sin (**Matthew 6:15**).

- **Judging Others**: Criticizing others for sins without repenting and turning from them ourselves is hypocrisy and sin (**Matthew 7:1-5**).

The Problem with Hypocrisy

We have a tendency to judge people for sins that differ from our own. We may point out the sins of others while neglecting to address our own faults. This hypocrisy creates a culture of judgment rather than grace and hinders our ability to reflect Christ's love.

Jesus warned against such hypocrisy in Matthew 7:1-5 (NIV): "Do not judge, or you too will be judged. In the same way you judge others, you will be judged, and the measure you use will be measured by you. Why do you look at the speck of sawdust in your brother's eye and pay no attention to the plank in your own eye? How can you say to your brother, 'Let me take the speck out of your eye,' when there is a plank in your own eye all the time? You hypocrite, first take the plank out of your own eye, and then you will see clearly to remove the speck from your brother's eye."

Jesus' teaching challenges us to examine our hearts and recognize our own sinfulness before passing judgment on others. Hypocrisy blinds us to our faults and prevents us from extending the grace and forgiveness we have received.

Embracing Humility and Grace

To overcome hypocrisy, we must embrace humility and grace. Humility involves recognizing our own need for forgiveness and acknowledging that we are all sinners in need of God's grace. Grace consists in extending love and understanding to others, even when they fall short.

James 4:6 (NIV) reminds us, "But he gives us more grace. That is why Scripture says: 'God opposes the proud but shows favor to the humble.'"

By embracing humility and grace, we align ourselves with God's heart and open the door to genuine transformation. Humility allows us to see others through God's eyes, recognizing their worth and potential for growth. Grace empowers us to love unconditionally and to support others in their journey toward Christ-likeness.

Anchoring Our Values in Christ

Jesus came to cleanse us of all our sins (**Romans 12:2**). Our focus should be on becoming more like Him, allowing His love and truth to transform us from the inside out. When we anchor our values in Christ, we become instruments of His grace and redemption in the world.

Anchoring our values in Christ requires a commitment to live according to His teachings and example. It means prioritizing love, mercy, and justice over judgment and condemnation. As we seek to embody Christ's character, we reflect His light and love to those around us.

Application

Reflect on your attitudes toward others. Are you quick to judge, or do you approach others with humility and grace? Consider how you can cultivate a heart that seeks to understand and support others in their spiritual journeys.

1. **Examine Your Heart**: Take time to reflect on your attitudes and actions toward others. Are you quick to judge, or do you approach others with empathy and understanding?

2. **Practice Self-Reflection**: Regularly assess your thoughts and behaviors, asking God to reveal any areas of hypocrisy in your life. Be willing to repent and seek His forgiveness and guidance.

3. **Cultivate Compassion**: Strive to see others through God's eyes, recognizing their worth and potential for growth. Extend grace and understanding, even when others fall short.

4. **Build Genuine Relationships**: Foster authentic connections with others by being vulnerable and transparent. Share your struggles and victories, and encourage others to do the same.

5. **Seek God's Guidance**: Spend time in prayer, asking God to reveal any areas of hypocrisy in your life and to help you align your actions with His love and truth. Ask Him to fill you with compassion and grace, enabling you to build meaningful relationships based on mutual respect and understanding.

Challenge Questions

1. How can you develop greater self-awareness and humility in your interactions with others, recognizing your own need for grace? Reflect on ways you can cultivate a humble heart and a willingness to learn from others.

2. In what ways can you extend grace and understanding to those who sin differently than you do, fostering an environment of acceptance and growth? Consider how you can create a safe space for others to share their struggles and seek support.

3. Reflect on a time when you experienced grace from someone else. How did that impact your life, and how can you extend that same grace to others? Use your experience to guide your interactions and encourage others.

By choosing humility and grace over hypocrisy and judgment, we create a community that reflects Christ's love and welcomes all people into the transformative power of His grace. As we seek to embody Christ's character, we become vessels of His love and truth, drawing others into a deeper relationship with Him.

Day 16:

Drink the Cup

In the world of leadership, there is a tendency to glamorize the role of spiritual leaders, painting a picture of privilege and luxury. However, authentic leadership in the Kingdom of God is marked by sacrifice, suffering, and a deep commitment to following Christ. Every true apostle and prophet has endured significant trials and hardships. These experiences shape and refine them, producing the character of Christ within.

The Cost of Leadership

The previous season of "rock star" leaders and green room speakers created a deceptive image of leadership as a glamorous lifestyle. Many aspire to this ideal, only to be surprised when they encounter the refining fires of adversity. The truth is that purity and character in leadership come at a cost. This cost is necessary to develop the depth and authenticity needed to lead others effectively.

Leadership in the Kingdom is not about personal gain or recognition but about serving others with humility and integrity. It requires a willingness to lay down one's life for the sake of the Gospel, to put aside personal ambitions, and to seek God's will above all else. This involves a radical shift in perspective, moving away from worldly notions of success and embracing the true essence of servant leadership as modeled by Jesus.

Mark 10:45 (NIV) states, "For even the Son of Man did not come to be served, but to serve, and to give his life as a ransom for many." Jesus' example sets the standard for all who aspire to lead in His name.

Pressing and Crushing

Leadership involves pressing, which produces oil, and crushing, which leads to death. These processes are essential to developing Christlike character. Just as olives must be pressed to release oil, so must leaders undergo pressure to cultivate purity and humility. This pressing is not meant to destroy but to transform, aligning our hearts with God's purposes.

The pressing process involves trials and challenges that test our faith and reveal our true character. It strips away superficialities and exposes areas in need of growth and refinement. Through these experiences, God works to purify our hearts, removing impurities and aligning our desires with His will.

2 Corinthians 4:8-9 (NIV) reminds us, "We are hard pressed on every side, but not crushed; perplexed, but not in despair; persecuted, but not abandoned; struck down, but not destroyed." This passage highlights the resilience and hope that come from trusting in God's sovereignty, even in the midst of trials.

Embracing Discipline and Warfare

Authentic leaders embrace the discipline of the Father and the warfare of satan and his demons. They understand that spiritual battles are a part of their calling and that God's discipline is a sign of His love and desire for their growth.

Hebrews 12:6 (NIV) says, "The Lord disciplines the one he loves, and he chastens everyone he accepts as his son." God's discipline is not punitive but corrective, designed to bring us into alignment with His will and to cultivate holiness in our lives.

Leaders also face betrayal, disappointment, slander, and accusations from people. These challenges test their resilience and drive them to rely on God's strength rather than their own. It is in these painful moments that they encounter God in profound ways, experiencing His comfort and guidance.

Psalm 34:19 (NIV) assures us, "The righteous person may have many troubles, but the Lord delivers him from them all." This promise reinforces the assurance that God is with us in our trials, providing strength and deliverance.

The Joy and Victory in Suffering

While suffering is part of the cup leaders must drink, it is accompanied by great joy and victory. The cup of suffering is not one of despair but of transformation and purpose. Leaders willingly drink this cup because they understand the eternal reward that awaits them—Jesus Christ Himself.

Suffering produces perseverance, character, and hope. It deepens our reliance on God and strengthens our faith, enabling us to withstand future challenges with resilience and courage.

Romans 5:3-5 (NIV) states, "Not only so, but we also glory in our sufferings because we know that suffering produces perseverance; perseverance, character; and character, hope. And hope does not put us to shame because God's love has been poured out into our hearts through the Holy Spirit, who has been given to us."

By pushing through the fear of man, leaders prioritize God's calling and remain focused on the accountability they will face before His throne. They recognize that their lives are ultimately lived for an audience of One, and they strive to finish the race with faithfulness and integrity.

Understanding the Call

To drink the cup is to say yes to God's call, fully aware of the challenges it entails. Jesus Himself set the example by embracing His suffering on the cross for the joy set before Him.

Hebrews 12:2 (NIV) encourages us, "Fixing our eyes on Jesus, the pioneer and perfecter of faith. For the joy set before him he endured the cross, scorning its shame, and sat down at the right hand of the throne of God."

Leaders are called to follow His example, understanding that the journey will not be easy but that the reward is worth every sacrifice. The call to leadership is a call to die to oneself, to take up the cross daily, and to serve others with the love and compassion of Christ.

Luke 9:23 (NIV) reminds us, "Whoever wants to be my disciple must deny themselves and take up their cross daily and follow me." This invitation challenges us to embrace the cost of discipleship and to commit fully to the mission of Christ.

Jesus is Worth It

Jesus is worth it. His presence, His love, and His promises far outweigh any earthly comfort or acclaim. When leaders embrace this truth, they find the courage and determination to persevere through trials and to lead others with grace and conviction.

The reward of leadership is not found in accolades or recognition but in the deep satisfaction of knowing that one has been faithful to God's call. It is in the quiet moments of communion with Christ that leaders find true joy and fulfill-ment.

Philippians 3:8-10 (NIV) captures this sentiment: "What is more, I consider everything a loss because of the surpassing worth of knowing Christ Jesus my Lord, for whose sake I have lost all things. I consider them garbage, that I may gain Christ and be found in him, not having a righteousness of my own that comes from the law, but that which is through faith in Christ—the righteousness that comes from God on the basis of faith."

Application

Reflect on your understanding of leadership. Are you prepared to embrace the cost of following Christ, including the challenges and sacrifices it may entail? Consider how you can develop a heart of perseverance and humility, relying on God's strength in times of adversity.

1. **Embrace the Process**: Accept that leadership involves challenges and sacrifices. Trust that God is using these experiences to shape your character and to equip you for greater impact.

2. **Cultivate Resilience**: Develop a mindset of perseverance and resilience, recognizing that God is with you in every trial. Lean on His strength and wisdom to navigate difficult situations.

3. **Prioritize God's Presence**: Spend time in prayer and wor-ship, seeking God's guidance and direction for your leadership journey. Allow His presence to refresh and sustain you.

4. **Seek God's Strength**: Spend time in prayer, asking God to reveal areas in your life where you need to grow in character and resilience. Invite Him to strengthen you for the journey ahead, trusting that He will equip you for every challenge.

Challenge Questions

1. How can you embrace the refining process of leadership, allowing God to shape your character through adversity? Reflect on the ways you can open yourself to God's transformative work in your life.

2. In what ways can you maintain focus on the eternal reward of Christ rather than seeking earthly recognition or comfort? Consider how you can align your priorities with God's purposes and keep your eyes fixed on Jesus.

3. Reflect on a time when you faced significant challenges in your leadership journey. How did God use those experiences to deepen your faith and reliance on Him? Use these reflections to guide your future leadership decisions and to inspire others.

By drinking the cup and saying yes to God's call, leaders commit to a path of transformation and purpose. They understand that the journey will be challenging but that the reward is eternal. Embrace the cost of leadership, trusting that God's grace will sustain you and that His presence is worth every sacrifice. As you lead with humility and faithfulness, may you reflect the heart of Christ and inspire others to follow in His footsteps.

Day 17:

Message to Young Preachers

In today's world, the availability of online sermons and teachings means that many Christians have favorite preachers they love to listen to. While these sermons can be inspiring, they often lack the personal touch and accountability that comes with having a shepherd to whom one can submit one's life. Young preachers, in particular, must learn to crave correction as much as inspiration in order to grow in their calling and effectively lead others.

The Challenge of Inspiration Without Correction

Inspiration is a powerful motivator. It can ignite passion, clarify vision, and motivate action. When young preachers are inspired, they often feel energized and ready to pursue their calling with zeal. Inspiration provides the initial spark that propels them forward, helping them envision what is possible in their ministry.

However, when young preachers rely solely on inspiration without seeking correction, they risk missing out on the profound growth and character development that come from being guided by a seasoned mentor or shepherd. Inspiration alone can lead to a superficial understanding of ministry, where the focus is on excitement rather than substance.

Proverbs 12:1 (NIV) states, "Whoever loves discipline loves knowledge, but whoever hates correction is stupid." This verse emphasizes the value of discipline and correction in gaining wisdom and understanding. It is through correction that young preachers can hone their skills, refine their messages, and align their lives with God's purposes.

Correction provides the necessary balance to inspiration, ensuring that young preachers remain grounded in truth and integrity. It is through the refining process of correction that they learn to handle the complexities of ministry with wisdom and discernment.

The Role of a Shepherd

A shepherd is more than just a preacher; a shepherd is someone who provides guidance, accountability, and care for their flock. A shepherd walks alongside their people, offering support and encouragement while also challenging them to grow in their faith and character.

While listening to sermons online can provide inspiration, having a shepherd offers a personal connection and accountability that cannot be achieved through distant teaching. A shepherd knows their flock intimately and can speak into their lives with insight and understanding.

Hebrews 13:17 (NIV) encourages believers to "have confidence in your leaders and submit to their authority because they keep watch over you as those who must give an account. Do this so that their work will be a joy, not a burden, for that would be of no benefit to you."

Young preachers need mentors who can speak truth into their lives, challenge them to grow, and hold them accountable in their ministry and personal walk with Christ. A mentor provides the wisdom and experience needed to navigate the challenges of leadership, offering guidance and support along the way.

The Importance of Craving Correction

Craving correction involves embracing humility and recognizing that growth often comes through uncomfortable but necessary feedback. Young preachers who are open to correction are more likely to develop into mature, effective leaders.

Proverbs 27:5-6 (NIV) states, "Better is open rebuke than hidden love. Wounds from a friend can be trusted, but an enemy multiplies kisses." Trusted mentors provide honest feedback that can be challenging but ultimately beneficial. Embracing correction demonstrates a willingness to learn and a commitment to becoming the best version of oneself in service to God and others.

Correction should not be viewed as a threat but as a valuable tool for growth. It is an opportunity to learn from mistakes, gain new perspectives, and refine one's approach to ministry. By welcoming correction, young preachers demonstrate a desire to pursue excellence and fulfill their calling with integrity.

Balancing Inspiration and Correction

Young preachers must strike a balance between seeking inspiration and embracing correction. Inspiration fuels passion and vision, while correction ensures alignment with God's truth and promotes character development.

James 1:22 (NIV) reminds us, "Do not merely listen to the word, and so deceive yourselves. Do what it says." Action based on inspiration is crucial, but it must be guided by wisdom and accountability. Correction helps ensure that actions align with biblical truth and are effective in fulfilling God's calling.

Finding this balance requires intentionality and discernment. Young preachers must be proactive in seeking both inspiration and correction, understanding that each plays a vital role in their development as leaders.

1. **Seek Inspiration**: Regularly engage with sermons, teachings, and resources that inspire and challenge you. Allow these messages to fuel your passion for ministry and to broaden your understanding of God's Word.

2. **Embrace Correction**: Surround yourself with mentors and peers who can provide honest feedback and constructive criticism. Be willing to listen and learn from their insights, recognizing that correction is a pathway to growth.

The Role of Mentors and Community

Mentors play a critical role in the development of young preachers. They offer guidance, support, and accountability, helping young leaders navigate the challenges of ministry with wisdom and grace.

1. **Guidance:** Mentors provide direction and advice, helping young preachers discern God's calling and develop a clear vision for their ministry. They offer practical insights based on their own experiences, helping young leaders avoid common pitfalls and make wise decisions.

2. **Support:** Mentors offer encouragement and support, walking alongside young preachers in their journey of faith. They provide a

safe space for young leaders to share their struggles, ask questions, and seek guidance.

3.   Accountability: Mentors hold young preachers accountable, challenging them to maintain integrity and to align their lives with biblical truth. They provide honest feedback and constructive criticism, helping young leaders grow in character and competence.

In addition to mentors, young preachers benefit from being part of a supportive community of peers and fellow leaders. This community provides opportunities for collaboration, learning, and mutual encouragement, fostering a sense of belonging and shared purpose.

Application

Young preachers should consider seeking out a mentor or shepherd who can provide guidance, accountability, and correction. Be open to feedback, and view correction as an opportunity for growth rather than a threat to your ego.

1.   Identify Mentors: Seek out individuals who exemplify the qualities of a godly leader and who can provide guidance and support in your ministry journey. Approach them with humility and a willingness to learn.

2.   Cultivate Relationships: Invest in relationships with mentors and peers who can offer constructive criticism and encouragement. Be intentional in building a community of support and accountability.

3.   Embrace Humility: Recognize that growth often comes through correction and that humility is essential for learning and development. Be willing to admit mistakes and seek guidance from others.

4.   Balance Inspiration and Correction: Regularly evaluate the sources of inspiration in your life and ensure they are balanced with meaningful accountability. Prioritize relationships with those who can offer constructive criticism and encourage you to grow in your calling.

Challenge Questions

1.   Who are the mentors or shepherds in your life who can provide guidance and correction? How can you strengthen those relationships? Reflect on the individuals who have influenced your journey and consider how you can deepen your connection with them.

2.   How can you create a healthy balance between seeking inspiration and embracing correction in your personal and ministry life? Evaluate your current approach and identify areas where you may need to adjust your focus or priorities.

3.   Reflect on a time when correction led to significant growth in your life. How can you continue to embrace correction as a tool for development and maturity? Consider how past experiences have shaped you and how you can apply those lessons moving forward.

By craving correction as much as inspiration, young preachers can develop into mature, influential leaders who are equipped to shepherd others and fulfill God's calling with integrity and grace. Embrace the opportunity to learn and grow, trusting that God will use your journey to impact others for His glory.

As you navigate the challenges and opportunities of ministry, remember that leadership is not about personal success or recognition but about serving others with humility and love. Allow inspiration to fuel your passion and vision, and let correction guide your growth and development. Through this balance, you will become a leader who reflects the heart of Christ and makes a lasting impact on the world.

Day 18:

How to Grow Leaders

Growing leaders is one of the most significant and rewarding responsibilities in any organization or community. The goal of leadership development is not to dictate the path others should take but to equip them to recognize and step into the opportunities God has already prepared for them. As leaders, our role is to show the way rather than make the way for them. This approach fosters independence, spiritual growth, and confidence among emerging leaders, allowing them to fulfill their God-given potential.

Show the Way, Don't Make the Way

The invitation to grow others should be rooted in demonstrating God's path and helping them develop the skills and discernment to walk in it. Jesus exemplified this approach in His relationship with His disciples. He did not plan their future in detail; instead, He prepared them for it by teaching them how to listen to God, understand His Word, and recognize His calling.

John 14:6 (NIV) reminds us of Jesus' teaching: "Jesus answered, 'I am the way and the truth and the life. No one comes to the Father except through me.'"

By pointing His disciples to Himself as the way, Jesus equipped them to find their own path through faith and obedience. He didn't give them a blueprint for their lives but provided them with the tools they needed to navigate their journeys. This approach encourages leaders to guide others to develop their own relationship with God, ensuring that their leadership is grounded in personal faith and conviction.

Prepare, Don't Plan

Leaders are called to prepare those they lead, not to plan every step of their journey. This involves equipping others with the knowledge, skills, and spiritual maturity they need to discern God's voice and direction.

Ephesians 4:11-13 (NIV) describes the purpose of spiritual leaders: "So Christ himself gave the apostles, the prophets, the evangelists, the pastors, and teachers, to equip his people for works of service, so that the body of Christ may be built up until we all reach unity in the faith and in the knowledge of the Son of God and become mature, attaining to the whole measure of the fullness of Christ."

Preparation focuses on developing the inner qualities necessary for effective leadership, such as integrity, humility, and a heart for service. It also involves teaching practical skills and fostering spiritual growth, enabling future leaders to step confidently into the roles God has designed for them.

Preparing leaders involves creating a supportive environment where they can explore their gifts, learn from their mistakes, and grow in their understanding of God's calling. This preparation empowers them to face challenges with resilience and to lead others with compassion and wisdom.

Recognize and Yield to Opportunities

As leaders, we are not solely responsible for creating opportunities for others but rather for helping them recognize and yield to the opportunities God presents. This requires discernment and the ability to guide others in recognizing God's timing and direction.

Proverbs 3:5-6 (NIV) advises, "Trust in the Lord with all your heart and lean not on your own understanding; in all your ways submit to him, and he will make your paths straight."

Encourage those you lead to trust God's guidance and to seek His will in every decision. Help them develop a strong foundation of faith and reliance on God's promises. By teaching them to listen to God's voice and to respond with obedience, we enable them to seize opportunities that align with His purposes.

Recognizing opportunities involves being attentive to the Holy Spirit's leading and being open to unexpected paths. Leaders should model this openness by sharing their own experiences of following God's guidance and trusting His plan.

Preparing for God's Path

Our role as leaders is to prepare others to step into the path God has already prepared for them. This involves nurturing their spiritual and personal development, providing opportunities for growth, and supporting them as they navigate challenges and opportunities.

Isaiah 30:21 (NIV) assures us, "Whether you turn to the right or to the left, your ears will hear a voice behind you, saying, 'This is the way; walk in it.'"

By fostering a culture of continuous learning and spiritual growth, we empower emerging leaders to listen to God's voice and to step into their God-given purpose with confidence and clarity. This preparation involves:

1. **Spiritual Growth**: Encourage regular study of Scripture, prayer, and worship, helping leaders deepen their relationship with God and grow in spiritual maturity.

2. **Skill Development**: Provide training and resources to help leaders develop the skills needed for their roles, such as communication, decision-making, and conflict resolution.

3. **Character Formation**: Emphasize the importance of character qualities like integrity, humility, and compassion, which are essential for effective leadership.

4. **Mentorship and Support**: Connect emerging leaders with mentors who can offer guidance, encouragement, and accountability as they navigate their leadership journey.

Application

Reflect on your approach to leadership development. Are you showing others the way and preparing them for God's path, or are you trying to plan every step for them? Consider how you can create an environment that encourages growth, discernment, and reliance on God's guidance.

1. **Empower Independence**: Encourage leaders to take initiative and make decisions based on their understanding of God's leading. Provide guidance and support, but allow them to learn from their experiences.

2. **Foster Community**: Create a supportive community where leaders can share their challenges and successes, learn from one another, and grow together in faith and leadership.

3. **Encourage Reflection**: Help leaders reflect on their experiences and discern how God is working in their lives. Encourage them to seek God's guidance and to trust His timing and direction.

Challenge Questions

1. **How can you shift your leadership approach from planning others' futures to preparing them to recognize and step into God's path?** Consider how you can empower others to take ownership of their leadership journey and to trust God's plan for their lives.

2. **In what ways can you create opportunities for those you lead to develop the skills and spiritual maturity needed for effective leadership?** Reflect on how you can provide training, resources, and support to help leaders grow in their roles.

3. **Reflect on a time when you were guided to recognize and yield to an opportunity God provided. How can you apply that experience to help others in their journeys?** Share your story with emerging leaders and encourage them to trust God's guidance in their own lives.

By focusing on preparation and guidance, we equip future leaders to navigate their unique paths with faith and purpose. Embrace the role of showing the way, trusting that God will lead them to the opportunities He has prepared.

Leadership is not about control or manipulation but about empowering others to discover and fulfill their God-given potential. As we invest in the development of leaders, we contribute to the growth of the Kingdom and the transformation of lives.

Through prayer, support, and intentional investment, we can raise up a generation of leaders who are equipped to impact the world for Christ. Let us commit to nurturing their growth and development, trusting that God will use their leadership to bring about His purposes on earth.

Day 19:

Cultural Perception

In a world where cultural norms and opinions constantly shift, it is easy to become swayed by prevailing views and societal pressures. However, just because something is widely accepted or proclaimed by culture does not make it accurate. This concept is humorously illustrated in a story about Abraham Lincoln, who once asked an audience how many legs a dog has if you count the tail as a leg. When they answered "five," Lincoln told them that the answer was four. The fact that you called the tail a leg did not make it a leg.

This story serves as a reminder that truth is not determined by popular opinion or cultural perception. Only God's Word is accurate, and it remains the standard by which we should measure all things.

The Illusion of Cultural Truth

Cultural perceptions are often shaped by trends, media, and influential voices. These perceptions can create an illusion of truth, leading people to accept ideas and practices that contradict God's Word. The danger lies in the subtlety of this influence; what is popular or widely accepted can quickly become perceived as truth.

In today's digital age, information is rapidly disseminated through social media and news outlets, shaping public opinion and influencing cultural norms. As believers, we must remain vigilant, recognizing that not everything presented as truth aligns with God's Word.

Romans 12:2 (NIV) warns against conforming to the patterns of this world: "Do not conform to the pattern of this world, but be transformed by the renewing of your mind. Then you will be able to test and approve what God's will is—his good, pleasing, and perfect will."

This verse highlights the importance of renewing our minds through God's Word so that we can discern His will and truth rather than being swayed by cultural norms. It calls us to be intentional about our thought processes, ensuring they are shaped by Scripture rather than societal pressures.

The Unchanging Truth of God's Word

Unlike cultural perceptions, God's Word is unchanging and eternal. It provides a solid foundation upon which we can build our lives. While cultural norms may shift with time, God's truth remains constant and reliable, offering guidance and wisdom for every aspect of life.

Isaiah 40:8 (NIV) affirms, "The grass withers and the flowers fall, but the word of our God endures forever."

God's truth is not subject to societal changes or human opinions. It stands firm, providing us with the direction and clarity needed to navigate the complexities of life. As believers, we are called to anchor our lives in this unchanging truth, allowing it to shape our beliefs, values, and actions.

Matthew 24:35 (NIV) further reinforces this concept: "Heaven and earth will pass away, but my words will never pass away." Jesus emphasizes that while everything around us may change, His words are eternal, serving as a steadfast guide through the shifting sands of cultural perception.

Grounding Our Beliefs in Truth

To navigate the shifting tides of cultural perception, we must anchor our beliefs in the unchanging truth of God's Word. This involves discerning what aligns with Scripture and rejecting what contradicts it. Grounding our beliefs, in fact, requires a commitment to studying Scripture, allowing it to shape our understanding of God's will and purposes.

Psalm 119:105 (NIV) declares, "Your word is a lamp for my feet, a light on my path."

God's Word illuminates our path, helping us to distinguish between truth and deception. It equips us to live in alignment with His purposes and to stand firm in our convictions, even when they differ from cultural norms. By immersing ourselves in Scripture, we develop the discernment needed to recognize falsehoods and to uphold God's truth in our lives.

2 Timothy 3:16-17 (NIV) underscores the value of Scripture in guiding our beliefs and actions: "All Scripture is God-breathed and is useful for teaching, rebuking, correcting and training in righteousness, so that the servant of God may be thoroughly equipped for every good work."

Courage to Stand for Truth

Standing for truth in a culture that values conformity requires courage and conviction. It may lead to criticism, misunderstanding, or even rejection. However, our commitment to God's truth is a testament to our faith and obedience. As believers, we are called to live out our convictions with integrity, trusting that God will honor our faithfulness.

1 Peter 3:15 (NIV) encourages us, "But in your hearts revere Christ as Lord. Always be prepared to give an answer to everyone who asks you to give the reason for the hope that you have. But do this with gentleness and respect."

As we engage with others, we must be prepared to share the truth of God's Word with gentleness and respect, offering a countercultural perspective grounded in love and wisdom. Our ability to articulate our beliefs with grace and humility reflects the character of Christ and opens doors for meaningful conversations.

Matthew 5:14-16 (NIV) calls us to be a light in the world: "You are the light of the world. A town built on a hill cannot be hidden. Neither do people light a lamp and put it under a bowl. Instead, they put it on its stand, and it gives light to everyone in the house. In the same way, let your light shine before others, that they may see your good deeds and glorify your Father in heaven."

By living out our faith with authenticity and courage, we become a beacon of truth and hope, pointing others to the unchanging love of God.

Application

Reflect on the cultural perceptions that influence your beliefs and values. Are there areas where you have conformed to societal norms rather than grounding your beliefs in God's truth? Consider how you can realign your perspective with Scripture.

1. **Evaluate Influences**: Take inventory of the media, relationships, and voices that shape your beliefs. Assess whether they align with God's truth or perpetuate cultural misconceptions.

2. **Renew Your Mind**: Commit to regular study of Scripture, allowing it to transform your mind and shape your worldview. Meditate on God's Word, seeking His guidance in every area of life.

3. **Pray for Wisdom**: Spend time in prayer, asking God to reveal areas where cultural perceptions have overshadowed His truth. Ask for the courage and wisdom to stand firm in your convictions, even when they are countercultural.

Challenge Questions

1. **How can you ensure that your beliefs and values are grounded in God's truth rather than cultural perceptions?** Reflect on your spiritual practices and consider how you can deepen your commitment to God's Word.

2. **In what ways can you be a light in your community, sharing God's truth with gentleness and respect?** Identify opportunities to engage in conversations that highlight the hope and love found in Christ.

3. **Reflect on a time when you faced pressure to conform to cultural norms. How did you respond, and what did you learn from that experience?** Consider how you can apply those lessons to future situations, trusting in God's strength and guidance.

By anchoring our beliefs in the unchanging truth of God's Word, we can navigate the complexities of cultural perception with confidence and clarity. Embrace the call to stand for truth, trusting that God's Word will guide and sustain you.

As we commit to living out our faith with integrity and courage, we become a testament to God's love and truth in a world hungry for hope and meaning. Let us hold fast to the eternal promises of God, allowing His Word to illuminate our path and empower us to make a lasting impact on His Kingdom.

Day 20:

Bees Don't Waste Their Time

In the pursuit of our dreams and callings, we often encounter people who doubt, criticize, or try to discourage us. However, much like bees who don't waste their time explaining to flies why honey is better than dung, we, too, should stay focused on our goals and not allow naysayers to derail us. This analogy reminds us to prioritize our purpose and let our actions speak louder than words.

Staying Focused on Your Purpose

Every individual is created with a unique purpose and calling. When we pursue our God-given dreams, we reflect His creativity and design. However, distractions and negativity from others can easily cause us to lose focus. It is essential to remain steadfast in our pursuit, trusting that God has a specific plan for each of us.

Proverbs 4:25-27 (NIV) advises, "Let your eyes look straight ahead; fix your gaze directly before you. Give careful thought to the paths for your feet and be steadfast in all your ways. Do not turn to the right or the left; keep your foot from evil."

This passage encourages us to remain focused on our path and to avoid distractions that can lead us astray. By fixing our gaze on our goals, we can navigate challenges with clarity and determination. Staying focused requires intentionality and discipline, ensuring that we do not waver in our commitment to God's calling.

Hebrews 12:1-2 (NIV) reinforces this idea: "Therefore since we are surrounded by such a great cloud of witnesses, let us throw off everything that hinders and the sin that so easily entangles. And let us run with perseverance the race marked out for us, fixing our eyes on Jesus, the pioneer and perfecter of faith."

By fixing our eyes on Jesus, we gain the strength and perseverance needed to fulfill our purpose, undeterred by the distractions and negativity around us.

Understanding the Nature of Naysayers

People who try to talk us out of our dreams often do so out of their own insecurities, fears, or limited perspectives. They may not understand the vision God has placed in our hearts, and their words can be more about their own limitations than about our potential. It is essential to recognize that their opinions do not define our worth or our calling.

Galatians 1:10 (NIV) reminds us, "Am I now trying to win the approval of human beings, or of God? Or am I trying to please people? If I were still trying to please people, I would not be a servant of Christ."

Our primary focus should be on pleasing God and fulfilling the calling He has placed on our lives rather than seeking the approval of others. When we prioritize God's opinion over that of others, we free ourselves from the need to justify our dreams to those who may not understand or support them.

1 Thessalonians 2:4 (NIV) echoes this sentiment: "We are not trying to please people but God, who tests our hearts."

Understanding that God alone knows the true desires and intentions of our hearts allows us to pursue our dreams with confidence and conviction, undeterred by the doubts or criticisms of others.

Embracing the Value of Honey

Just as bees recognize the value of honey, we, too, should recognize the worth of our dreams and callings. Honey, in this analogy, represents the sweetness and fulfillment that come from pursuing our God-given purpose. It is the reward of diligence, perseverance, and faith.

Ecclesiastes 3:13 (NIV) states, "That each of them may eat and drink, and find satisfaction in all their toil—this is the gift of God."

Finding satisfaction and fulfillment in our work is a gift from God, and it serves as a testament to His provision and faithfulness. When we embrace the value of our dreams, we are motivated to pursue them with dedication and passion, trusting that God will provide the resources and opportunities needed to achieve them.

Colossians 3:23-24 (NIV) encourages us, "Whatever you do, work at it with all your heart, as working for the Lord, not for human masters, since you know that you will receive an inheritance from the Lord as a reward."

When we work diligently for the Lord, we are assured of His blessings and rewards, which far surpass any earthly recognition or acclaim.

Letting Actions Speak

Rather than engaging in fruitless debates or trying to justify our dreams to those who doubt us, we should let our actions and achievements speak for themselves. Like bees who continue to produce honey regardless of what flies think, we should focus on the work at hand and trust that our efforts will bear fruit.

1 Peter 2:15 (NIV) encourages us, "For it is God's will that by doing good you should silence the ignorant talk of foolish people."

Our commitment to our purpose and the excellence with which we pursue it can serve as a powerful testimony to others. When our actions align with God's will, they become a reflection of His love and truth, influencing those around us more effectively than words alone ever could.

James 2:18 (NIV) further supports this idea: "But someone will say, 'You have faith; I have deeds.' Show me your faith without deeds, and I will show you my faith by my deeds."

Our actions are a demonstration of our faith and commitment to God's calling, serving as a witness to His transformative power in our lives.

Application

Reflect on the areas in your life where you have allowed the opinions of others to deter you from pursuing your dreams. Consider how you can refocus your attention on God's calling and remain steadfast in your purpose.

1. **Identify Distractions**: Take note of the people, situations, or thoughts that have distracted you from your goals. Evaluate whether these influences align with God's calling for your life.

2. **Refocus Your Gaze**: Recommit to pursuing your God-given dreams with focus and determination. Set clear goals and create a plan to achieve them, seeking God's guidance at every step.

3. **Pray for Strength**: Spend time in prayer, asking God to strengthen your resolve and to help you discern His guidance for your life. Seek His wisdom in navigating criticism and staying true to the path He has set before you.

Challenge Questions

1. **How can you remain focused on your God-given calling and avoid being distracted by naysayers?** Consider practical steps you can take to maintain your focus, such as setting boundaries or seeking accountability from trusted mentors.

2. **In what ways can you demonstrate the value of your dreams through your actions and achievements?** Reflect on how your work can serve as a testament to God's provision and faithfulness, inspiring others to pursue their own callings.

3. **Reflect on a time when you overcame criticism to pursue your dreams. How did that experience strengthen your faith and commitment?** Consider the lessons learned from that experience and how they can be applied to future challenges.

By staying focused on our calling and letting our actions speak, we can fulfill the purpose God has given us and experience the sweetness of a life lived in alignment with His will. Embrace your dreams and pursue them with confidence, knowing that God is with you every step of the way.

Trust in His guidance and provision, and let your life be a testimony to His love and faithfulness. As you remain committed to your purpose, you will inspire others to do the same, contributing to the growth of God's Kingdom and the transformation of lives.

Day 21:

Relationships are Wells

In the journey of life, relationships are like wells. They provide nourishment, refreshment, and sustenance. However, just as it is much easier to poison a well than to dig one, maintaining healthy relationships requires effort and intentionality. Those who work to build meaningful connections often face challenges from those who seek to undermine or sabotage their efforts. Remember, the people trying to poison your well probably haven't dug much themselves.

The Importance of Building Relationships

Building solid relationships is an essential aspect of a fulfilling and meaningful life. Just as a well provides water to sustain physical life, relationships offer emotional, spiritual, and social support. They are sources of encouragement, accountability, and love, helping us to navigate the complexities of life. Relationships are crucial for personal growth and spiritual development, offering a network of support that allows us to become the people God intends us to be.

Proverbs 27:17 (NIV) states, "As iron sharpens iron, so one person sharpens another."

This verse emphasizes the mutual benefit of relationships, where individuals grow and strengthen each other through their interactions. By investing in relationships, we create a network of support and growth that enhances our lives and the lives of those around us. Strong relationships are the foundation of a thriving community where people uplift and encourage one another in their journeys.

Ecclesiastes 4:9-10 (NIV) further highlights the importance of relationships: "Two are better than one, because they have a good return for their labor: If either of them falls down, one can help the other up. But pity anyone who falls and has no one to help them up."

This passage reminds us that we are not meant to journey through life alone. Relationships provide the support we need in times of difficulty and celebrate with us in times of joy.

The Challenge of Poisoning

Despite the importance of healthy relationships, it is easier to poison a well than to dig one. Poisoning represents the negative influences and destructive behaviors that can damage relationships. This can take the form of gossip, jealousy, criticism, or betrayal, which can undermine trust and intimacy. These actions are often rooted in insecurity, fear, or a desire to control, and they can have devastating effects on relationships.

James 3:5-6 (NIV) warns about the power of the tongue: "Likewise, the tongue is a small part of the body, but it makes great boasts. Consider what a great forest is set on fire by a small spark. The tongue also is a fire, a world of evil among the parts of the body."

Words have the power to build up or tear down relationships. Being mindful of our words and actions is crucial to protecting the wells we have worked hard to dig. A careless word or thoughtless action can cause significant harm, and once trust is broken, it can be challenging to rebuild.

Proverbs 16:28 (NIV) also highlights the destructive potential of negative words: "A perverse person stirs up conflict, and gossip separates close friends."

To safeguard our relationships, we must be vigilant against these negative influences and strive to foster an environment of trust and respect.

The Value of Well Diggers

Those who invest in building and maintaining relationships are like well diggers. They understand the effort required to create and sustain meaningful connections. Well diggers are intentional about nurturing relationships, investing time, energy, and love into building a solid foundation. They prioritize understanding, empathy, and communication, recognizing that strong relationships are built on mutual respect and care.

Romans 12:10 (NIV) encourages us, "Be devoted to one another in love. Honor one another above yourselves."

Well diggers prioritize love and honor in their relationships, recognizing the value of putting others first and building each other up. They seek to create an atmosphere where everyone feels valued and appreciated, fostering a sense of belonging and community.

Philippians 2:3-4 (NIV) further emphasizes the importance of humility and selflessness in relationships: "Do nothing out of selfish ambition or vain conceit. Rather, in humility, value others above yourselves, not looking to your own interests but each of you to the interests of the others."

By prioritizing the well-being of others, well-diggers create a culture of generosity and kindness that strengthens relationships and builds community.

Navigating Challenges and Sabotage

Unfortunately, not everyone appreciates or supports the efforts of well diggers. People who try to poison wells often lack the experience or willingness to invest in meaningful relationships themselves. Their actions may stem from insecurity, envy, or a desire to exert control. In such situations, well diggers must remain steadfast in their commitment to building healthy relationships, responding to negativity with grace and integrity.

1 Peter 3:9 (NIV) advises, "Do not repay evil with evil or insult with insult. On the contrary, repay evil with blessing, because to this you were called so that you may inherit a blessing."

When faced with sabotage or negativity, well diggers should respond with grace and integrity, maintaining their commitment to building healthy relationships. By choosing kindness and understanding, they can defuse tension and promote healing, transforming potential conflicts into opportunities for growth and reconciliation.

Matthew 5:44 (NIV) further instructs us to love our enemies and pray for those who persecute us. By embodying this principle, well diggers can foster a spirit of forgiveness and understanding, even in challenging situations.

Application

Reflect on the relationships in your life. Are you a good digger, investing in meaningful connections, or have you allowed negativity to poison your wells?

Consider how you can nurture and protect your relationships, fostering an environment of love and growth.

1. **Evaluate Your Relationships**: Take stock of your relationships and identify areas where negativity or misunderstandings may have taken root. Consider how you can address these issues with grace and compassion, seeking to restore and strengthen your connections.

2. **Commit to Growth**: Dedicate yourself to personal growth and development, recognizing that healthy relationships require effort and intentionality. Seek to improve your communication skills, empathy, and understanding, fostering an environment of trust and respect.

3. **Pray for Wisdom**: Spend time in prayer, asking God for wisdom and discernment in your relationships. Seek His guidance in navigating challenges and building connections that honor Him and reflect His love.

Challenge Questions

1. **How can you become more intentional about building and maintaining healthy relationships in your life?** Consider practical steps you can take to invest in your relationships, such as setting aside regular time for meaningful conversations and activities with loved ones.

2. **In what ways can you respond to negativity or sabotage with grace and integrity, protecting the wells you have worked hard to dig?** Reflect on strategies for addressing conflict and negativity, such as active listening, empathy, and seeking common ground.

3. **Reflect on a relationship where you have experienced growth and mutual support. How can you continue to invest in that relationship and encourage others to do the same?** Identify opportunities for further strengthening your connections, such as expressing appreciation, offering support, and sharing experiences.

By choosing to be well-diggers, we create relationships that nourish and sustain us, reflecting God's love and grace to those around us. Embrace the challenge of building meaningful connections, trusting that your efforts will lead to deeper, more fulfilling relationships. As we commit to investing in others, we not only enrich our own lives but also contribute to the growth and well-being of our communities, fostering a spirit of love and unity that reflects the heart of God.

Day 22:

What Spiritual Maturity Is

Spiritual maturity is a vital aspect of our journey as believers. It's essential to recognize that maturity is not an age thing—it doesn't automatically come as we get older. Instead, maturity is a growth thing. It is a continual process of transformation, requiring intentional effort and openness to God's work in our lives. True maturity is characterized by ongoing growth, self-awareness, and the ability to reflect Christ's character.

Maturity is Not Just Age

Many people mistakenly equate maturity with age, assuming that simply growing older brings about wisdom and depth. However, age alone does not guarantee maturity. It is possible to age without growing, remaining stagnant in our spiritual and personal development. True maturity is not measured by the number of years we have lived but by the depth of our relationship with God and the fruit we produce in our lives.

Hebrews 5:12-14 (NIV) highlights this point: "In fact, though by this time you ought to be teachers, you need someone to teach you the elementary truths of God's word all over again. You need milk, not solid food! Anyone who lives on milk, being still an infant, is not acquainted with the teaching about righteousness. But solid food is for the mature, who by constant use have trained themselves to distinguish good from evil."

This passage emphasizes the need for believers to move beyond the basics and to pursue a deeper understanding of God's Word and His ways. Maturity requires active engagement in learning and growing, allowing God to refine us and shape us into His image. It involves a commitment to continual growth and the willingness to embrace God's transformative work in our lives.

The Traits of Spiritual Maturity

Spiritual maturity involves continuous growth and transformation. It means recognizing that we have not "arrived" and always seeking to deepen our relationship with God and others. The traits of spiritual maturity are evident in the way we live, interact with others, and respond to challenges.

1. **Growth Over Time**: Maturity is an ongoing process. We must constantly seek to grow in our faith and understanding, allowing God to refine us and shape us into His image. This involves a commitment to spiritual disciplines such as prayer, Bible study, and fellowship with other believers, which foster spiritual growth and maturity.

2. **Self-Awareness**: True maturity involves recognizing our imperfections and taking responsibility for our growth. It means refusing to excuse our flaws as "just who we are" but instead striving to overcome them through God's grace and power. Self-awareness allows us to identify areas where we need to grow and to seek God's help in overcoming our weaknesses.

3. **Humility and Restraint**: Maturity is evident when we can be right without needing to prove it or hold others hostage to our opinions. It involves listening to others, valuing their perspectives, and acknowledging that we do not have to be the only voice in the room to know our worth. Humility allows us to learn from others and to appreciate the contributions they make to our lives.

Philippians 2:3-4 (NIV) encourages us, "Do nothing out of selfish ambition or vain conceit. Rather, in humility, value others above yourselves, not looking to your own interests but each of you to the interests of the others."

This passage highlights the importance of humility and selflessness in our relationships with others. Mature individuals prioritize the needs of others and seek to build others up, fostering an environment of mutual respect and love.

4. **Peacemaking**: Mature individuals are peace bringers, not strife stirrers. They seek to build unity and harmony, using their words and actions to uplift and encourage others. Peacemaking involves addressing conflicts with grace and understanding, seeking resolution and reconciliation rather than division.

Matthew 5:9 (NIV) declares, "Blessed are the peacemakers, for they will be called children of God."

This beatitude emphasizes the importance of peacemaking as a reflection of our identity as God's children. Mature believers are committed to fostering peace and unity in their relationships and communities.

The Pitfalls of False Maturity

Some people think they are mature because they have learned to disguise their immaturity with religious undertones or socially acceptable behaviors. They may talk about people, practice escapism, entertain damaging thoughts, or stir strife, all while maintaining an appearance of maturity. False maturity is characterized by a lack of authenticity and integrity, where individuals prioritize appearances over genuine growth and transformation.

Matthew 7:16-17 (NIV) warns, "By their fruit, you will recognize them. Do people pick grapes from thornbushes or figs from thistles? Likewise, every good tree bears good fruit, but a bad tree bears bad fruit."

True maturity is revealed by the fruit we produce, reflecting the character and love of Christ in all we do. Our actions, attitudes, and relationships are evidence of our maturity, demonstrating the depth of our faith and commitment to God's purposes.

Galatians 5:22-23 (NIV) describes the fruit of the Spirit as "love, joy, peace, forbearance, kindness, goodness, faithfulness, gentleness and self-control."

These qualities are the hallmark of spiritual maturity, reflecting the transformative work of the Holy Spirit in our lives. Mature believers are characterized by their love for others, their joy and peace in all circumstances, and their commitment to living out their faith with integrity and grace.

The Importance of Continual Growth

Maturity is not a destination but a journey. It requires intentional effort and a willingness to grow and change. We must be open to God's refining work in our lives, allowing Him to strip away the things that hinder our growth and cultivate His character within us. Continual growth involves a commitment to learning and development, seeking to deepen our relationship with God and to live out our faith in practical ways.

2 Peter 3:18 (NIV) encourages us to "grow in the grace and knowledge of our Lord and Savior Jesus Christ."

By pursuing growth and maturity, we become more effective instruments of God's love and grace in the world. Our maturity allows us to navigate challenges with wisdom and discernment, build meaningful relationships, and contribute to the growth and well-being of our communities.

Application

Reflect on your spiritual journey. Are you actively seeking growth, or have you become complacent in your development? Consider how you can deepen your relationship with God and others, embracing the traits of true maturity.

1. **Pursue Spiritual Disciplines**: Commit to regular practices such as prayer, Bible study, and fellowship with other believers. These disciplines foster spiritual growth and maturity, providing opportunities for reflection, learning, and development.

2. **Seek Accountability**: Surround yourself with mature believers who can offer guidance, encouragement, and accountability in your spiritual journey. Seek out mentors and role models who exemplify the qualities of spiritual maturity and who can support you in your growth.

3. **Embrace Change**: Be open to God's refining work in your life, recognizing that growth often involves change and transformation. Be willing to let go of habits, attitudes, and behaviors that hinder your development and embrace new opportunities for growth and learning.

Challenge Questions

1. How can you cultivate a mindset of continuous growth and transformation in your spiritual journey? Consider practical steps you can take to foster growth, such as setting goals, seeking feedback, and engaging in spiritual practices that challenge and stretch you.

2. In what areas of your life do you need to practice humility and restraint, valuing others' perspectives and contributions? Reflect on how you can prioritize the needs and well-being of others, demonstrating humility and selflessness in your relationships and interactions.

3. Reflect on a time when you witnessed true spiritual maturity in someone else. How did their example inspire you, and how can you apply those lessons to your own life? Consider how you can emulate their qualities and behaviors, seeking to embody the traits of spiritual maturity in your own life.

By pursuing spiritual maturity, we align ourselves with God's purposes and become vessels of His love and truth. Embrace the journey of growth, trusting that God will transform you into the person He created you to be. As we commit to ongoing growth and development, we become more effective witnesses to His love and grace, contributing to the transformation of our communities and the advancement of His Kingdom.

Day 23:

Defining an Old Wineskin

In our spiritual journey, we are often called to embrace change and renewal as God continues to work in new and dynamic ways. However, there is a tendency to cling to the familiar and resist the fresh move of God. This resistance creates what Jesus referred to as "old wineskins," which are unable to contain the new wine of His Spirit. Understanding and recognizing these old wineskins is crucial for experiencing the fullness of God's work in our lives.

Understanding Old Wineskins

Old wineskins represent a mindset or structure that has become rigid and inflexible. In ancient times, new wine was poured into fresh wineskins because they were pliable and could expand with the fermentation process. Old wineskins, on the other hand, were brittle and unable to stretch, leading to them bursting when filled with new wine. The concept of old wineskins symbolizes the danger of becoming spiritually rigid and resistant to change, preventing us from receiving the fresh outpouring of God's Spirit.

Mark 2:22 (NIV) explains this concept: "And no one pours new wine into old wineskins. Otherwise, the wine will burst the skins, and both the wine and the wineskins will be ruined. No, they pour new wine into new wineskins."

Jesus used this metaphor to illustrate the importance of being open to God's ongoing work and willing to embrace change. Old wineskins are a reminder of the necessity to remain flexible and adaptable in our spiritual journey, allowing God to transform us and fill us with His new wine.

Identifying Old Wineskins in Our Lives

Old wineskins can take various forms in our spiritual lives. Here are some key indicators of old wineskins:

1. **Settling for the Last Move of God**: Anytime we pay for what God has done in the past and resist His present work, we become like old wineskins. God is constantly moving and calling us to new lev-

els of faith and obedience. Clinging to past experiences can hinder our ability to perceive and respond to God's current work in our lives.

2. Preserving the Past: When we seek to protect and preserve past experiences with God while ignoring or suppressing what He is currently doing, we hinder spiritual growth and renewal. God's work is dynamic, and He desires to lead us into new experiences and revelations.

Isaiah 43:18-19 (NIV) encourages us: "Forget the former things; do not dwell on the past. See, I am doing a new thing! Now it springs up; do you not perceive it?"

This passage challenges us to recognize and embrace the new work God is doing, moving beyond our comfort zones and expectations.

3. Choosing Tradition Over Truth: Traditions can be valuable, but when they take precedence over God's truth, they become a hindrance to spiritual progress. True faith is not bound by tradition but is responsive to God's ongoing revelation. We must be willing to question and reassess traditions in light of God's truth and revelation.

4. Prioritizing Religion Over Revelation: Anytime we choose religious practices and rituals over a genuine relationship with God, we limit the work of the Holy Spirit in our lives. God desires intimacy and authenticity, not mere religious performance. Our faith should be characterized by a vibrant relationship with God, grounded in His Word and Spirit.

5. Maintaining the Status Quo: Choosing the comfort of the status quo over a holy hunger for more of God leads to stagnation. Spiritual growth requires a willingness to step out of our comfort zones and pursue deeper intimacy with God. We must be open to God's leading, willing to embrace the unknown and trust His guidance.

6. Relying on Skills and Programs: When we prioritize our skills, programs, and human efforts over-reliance on the Holy Spirit, we miss out on the supernatural work God wants to accomplish through us. God's power is made perfect in our weakness, and we must be willing to rely on Him rather than our own abilities.

Embracing New Wineskins

To receive the new wine of God's Spirit, we must become new wineskins—flexible, open, and ready to receive all that God has for us. This involves a willingness to let go of old patterns, beliefs, and practices that no longer serve His purposes. Embracing new wineskins requires a mindset of openness and a heart ready for transformation.

Romans 12:2 (NIV) encourages us, "Do not conform to the pattern of this world but be transformed by the renewing of your mind. Then you will be able to test and approve what God's will is—his good, pleasing, and perfect will."

Transformation begins with a renewed mind and a heart open to God's leading. By embracing new wineskins, we position ourselves to experience the fullness of God's work in our lives, allowing His Spirit to lead and guide us.

The Role of Openness and Flexibility

Openness and flexibility are vital to embracing new wineskins. We must be willing to let go of rigid thinking and be open to God's new and unexpected ways. This means being willing to question our assumptions, seek God's guidance, and be receptive to His leadership.

Proverbs 3:5-6 (NIV) advises, "Trust in the Lord with all your heart and lean not on your own understanding; in all your ways submit to him, and he will make your paths straight."

Trusting God involves relinquishing control and being open to His direction, even when it challenges our preconceived notions and comfort zones.

Application

Reflect on areas in your life where you may have become an old wineskin, resistant to God's new work. Consider how you can open yourself to His fresh move and become a vessel for His Spirit. Embrace the process of renewal and transformation, allowing God to work in and through you.

1.   **Examine Your Heart**: Take time to reflect on areas where you may be resisting change or clinging to old patterns. Ask God to reveal any areas of rigidity or inflexibility in your life.

2.   **Seek God's Guidance**: Spend time in prayer, seeking God's wisdom and direction. Ask Him to help you discern His new work and to give you the courage to embrace it.

3.   **Be Willing to Change**: Be open to change and willing to let go of old ways that no longer serve God's purposes. Trust that God's new wine will bring life and vitality to your spiritual journey.

Challenge Questions

1. How can you become more receptive to God's new work and avoid becoming an old wineskin in your spiritual journey? Consider practical steps you can take to cultivate openness and flexibility, such as seeking new experiences, engaging with diverse perspectives, and being willing to learn and grow.

2. In what ways can you prioritize God's truth and revelation over tradition and religion in your life? Reflect on how you can align your beliefs and practices with God's Word and Spirit, allowing His truth to guide your actions and decisions.

3. Reflect on a time when you experienced God's new work in a powerful way. How did it impact your faith, and how can you continue to embrace His fresh move? Consider how you can continue to seek and embrace God's ongoing work in your life, trusting that He will lead you into greater depths of faith and intimacy.

By choosing to be new wineskins, we open ourselves to the dynamic and transformative work of the Holy Spirit. Embrace the call to renewal, trusting that God's new wine will bring fresh life and vitality to your spiritual journey. As we remain open and flexible, we position ourselves to experience the fullness of God's purposes and to become vessels of His love and grace in the world. Let us be willing to embrace change and trust in God's leading, knowing that He is always at work, bringing about new and more significant things in our lives.

Day 24:

How to Hear God's Voice

Hearing God's voice is a vital part of our spiritual journey. It allows us to receive guidance, wisdom, and encouragement directly from our Creator. However, discerning God's voice amidst the noise and distractions of life can be challenging. To cultivate a deeper relationship with God and hear His voice more clearly, we must develop intentional practices that help us tune into His presence and guidance. Here are several practical steps to help you cultivate the ability to hear God's voice more clearly.

1.   Open the Bible

The Word of God is God-breathed and serves as the foundation for understanding His voice. The Bible is the primary way God speaks to us, providing wisdom, guidance, and truth for every situation. Engaging with Scripture regularly is essential for recognizing God's voice and aligning our lives with His will.

2 Timothy 3:16-17 (NIV) reminds us, "All Scripture is God-breathed and is useful for teaching, rebuking, correcting, and training in righteousness, so that the servant of God may be thoroughly equipped for every good work."

By regularly reading and meditating on Scripture, we align our hearts and minds with God's truth, making it easier to recognize His voice when He speaks. The Bible equips us with the knowledge and understanding necessary to discern God's will and respond to His leading.

2.   Listen to the Holy Spirit

The Holy Spirit speaks to our spirit through promptings, impressions, suggestions, dreams, and visions. He provides guidance and insight into God's will for our lives, helping us navigate the complexities of daily living.

John 16:13 (NIV) states, "But when he, the Spirit of truth, comes, he will guide you into all the truth."

Cultivating sensitivity to the Holy Spirit's leading involves prayer, reflection, and openness to His direction. Pay attention to the subtle nudges and insights

He provides throughout your day. The Holy Spirit is our counselor and guide, leading us into deeper understanding and communion with God.

3. Pay Attention to Peace

God's voice brings peace. If you don't have peace about something, it may be God speaking to you. His peace acts as a compass, guiding us toward His will and confirming His direction in our lives.

Colossians 3:15 (NIV) encourages us, "Let the peace of Christ rule in your hearts, since as members of one body you were called to peace."

When making decisions, seek God's peace as confirmation of His direction and trust that He will lead you on the right path. Peace is a fruit of the Spirit and a sign of God's presence in our lives. It reassures us that we are aligned with His will and walking in His ways.

4. Lower the Noise in Your Life

To hear God more clearly, we must lower the noise and distractions in our lives. This involves setting aside time for silence, reflection, and prayer, allowing space for God to speak. In our busy world, creating moments of stillness is essential for cultivating a deeper connection with God.

Psalm 46:10 (NIV) instructs us, "Be still, and know that I am God."

Create intentional moments of stillness in your day, silencing external and internal distractions to focus on God's presence. Practice mindfulness and solitude, allowing your heart and mind to be open to His voice.

5. Obey What God Told You Before

If you don't heed God's voice, you may stop hearing it over time. Obedience to God's previous instructions opens the door for further revelation. When we act on what God has already revealed, we demonstrate our faithfulness and readiness to receive more of His guidance.

James 1:22 (NIV) advises, "Do not merely listen to the word, and so deceive yourselves. Do what it says."

Acting on what God has already revealed demonstrates faithfulness and readiness to receive more of His guidance. Obedience is a critical component of spiritual growth and a reflection of our commitment to follow God's will.

6. God Can Speak Through Confirming Circumstances

God often uses circumstances to confirm His voice and direction. When things fall into place, it can be a sign that God is speaking and guiding you. Pay attention to how events unfold in your life and be open to recognizing God's hand in orchestrating circumstances.

Proverbs 16:9 (NIV) states, "In their hearts, humans plan their course, but the Lord establishes their steps."

Look for patterns and signs that align with God's Word and the promptings of the Holy Spirit. God's sovereignty is evident in the way He orchestrates events and circumstances to guide us along His path.

7. Listen to Trusted Mentors and Prophets

God uses others to speak to us. Trusted mentors and prophets can provide insight, encouragement, and confirmation of God's voice. Surround yourself with wise and spiritually mature individuals who can help you discern God's voice and direction.

Proverbs 11:14 (NIV) reminds us, "For lack of guidance a nation falls, but victory is won through many advisers."

Seek counsel from those who have a deep relationship with God and who can offer wisdom and perspective. Their guidance can help you navigate challenges and confirm the path God is leading you on.

Application

Reflect on your current practices for hearing God's voice. Are there areas where you can grow in sensitivity and discernment? Consider implementing these steps into your daily routine to enhance your ability to hear God's voice clearly. Cultivating a deep and intimate relationship with God requires intentional effort and a willingness to listen.

Challenge Questions

1. How can you create more opportunities for stillness and silence in your life to hear God's voice more clearly? Consider setting aside specific times for prayer and reflection each day, eliminating distractions, and focusing on God's presence.

2. In what ways can you cultivate sensitivity to the Holy Spirit's promptings and guidance? Explore practices such as journaling, meditation, and spiritual disciplines that enhance your awareness of the Holy Spirit's leading.

3. Reflect on a time when you clearly heard God's voice. What practices helped you discern His guidance, and how can you continue to develop those habits? Identify the factors that contributed to your ability to hear God and seek to integrate those practices into your daily life.

By seeking to hear God's voice, we draw closer to Him and align our lives with His purposes. Embrace the journey of listening and responding to His guidance, trusting that He will lead you on the path He has prepared.

Hearing God's voice is an ongoing process that requires intentionality, openness, and a willingness to follow His lead. As we cultivate practices that enhance our ability to hear God, we grow in intimacy with Him and align our lives with His purposes. Embrace the journey of listening and responding to God's voice, trusting that He will guide you with wisdom and love.

In a world filled with noise and distractions, the ability to hear God's voice is a precious gift that draws us closer to Him and empowers us to live out His calling. By following these steps and remaining open to God's leading, we can cultivate a deeper, more intimate relationship with our Creator and experience the joy and fulfillment that comes from walking in His will.

Day 25:

When Bad Decisions Are Made

Life is full of decisions, and sometimes, we make choices that lead to undesirable outcomes. Reflecting on these decisions, we often realize that they were influenced by our emotional state at the time. Recognizing the factors that lead to poor decisions can help us develop strategies to make wiser choices in the future. Understanding our emotional triggers and seeking God's guidance is crucial to making decisions that align with His will and our long-term goals.

Recognizing the Triggers of Bad Decisions

As I look back over my life, I realize that I have made my worst decisions when I am scared, bored, hurt, or tired. These emotional states cloud our judgment and can lead us to make choices that do not align with our values or long-term goals. Identifying these triggers is the first step toward making better decisions.

When I Am Scared

Fear can be a powerful motivator, often leading us to make impulsive or irrational decisions. When fear takes hold, we may act out of a desire to protect ourselves or avoid perceived threats rather than make thoughtful choices. Fear can distort our perception, causing us to react in ways that are not in line with God's truth and love.

Isaiah 41:10 (NIV) encourages us, "So do not fear, for I am with you; do not be dismayed, for I am your God. I will strengthen you and help you; I will uphold you with my righteous right hand."

This verse reminds us that God's presence and strength are available to us in times of fear. When fear arises, we must remember that God is with us and that He will provide the strength and guidance we need to make wise decisions. Instead of reacting out of fear, we can pause, seek God's peace, and trust Him to lead us on the right path.

When I Am Bored

Boredom can lead to restlessness and a desire for excitement or change, prompting us to make hasty decisions that may not be in our best interest. When we are bored, we may seek temporary relief through impulsive actions without considering the long-term consequences.

Proverbs 19:2 (NIV) warns, "Desire without knowledge is not good—how much more will hasty feet miss the way!"

It is essential to seek purposeful activities and pursuits that align with our goals and values rather than making impulsive decisions to fill the void of boredom. By engaging in meaningful work, hobbies, and relationships, we can find fulfillment and purpose that satisfy our deeper needs.

When I Am Hurt

Emotional pain can distort our perception and lead to decisions driven by a desire to numb or escape the hurt. In these moments, we may choose actions that provide temporary relief but ultimately compound our suffering. Hurt can lead to a cycle of negative emotions and reactions that distance us from God's healing and grace.

Psalm 34:18 (NIV) assures us, "The Lord is close to the brokenhearted and saves those who are crushed in spirit."

Instead of making decisions in response to pain, we can turn to God for comfort and healing, allowing Him to guide us in making choices that lead to wholeness and restoration. By seeking God's presence and love, we can find the strength to face our pain and make decisions that honor Him and promote healing.

When I Am Tired

Fatigue diminishes our ability to think clearly and make rational decisions. When we are tired, we may take shortcuts or opt for easy solutions that are not in line with our values or long-term objectives. Tiredness can lead to a lack of focus and discernment, causing us to compromise our integrity and goals.

Matthew 11:28 (NIV) invites us, "Come to me, all you who are weary and burdened, and I will give you rest."

Rest and renewal are essential for making wise decisions. By prioritizing self-care and seeking God's strength, we can make choices that reflect His wisdom and love. Taking time to rest and recharge allows us to approach decisions with clarity and intention, aligning our actions with God's will.

Turning Mistakes into Learning Opportunities

A mistake repeated more than once is not a mistake; it's a decision. Recognizing patterns in our decision-making allows us to identify areas for growth and improvement. Rather than condemning ourselves for past mistakes, we can learn from them and seek God's guidance in making better choices moving forward.

James 1:5 (NIV) offers us this promise: "If any of you lacks wisdom, you should ask God, who gives generously to all without finding fault, and it will be given to you."

God is eager to provide the wisdom we need to navigate life's challenges and make decisions that honor Him. By turning to God in prayer and seeking His guidance, we can transform our mistakes into opportunities for growth and transformation.

Application

Reflect on past decisions and identify the emotional states that influenced them. Consider how you can develop strategies to manage these emotions and make wiser choices in the future. By understanding the triggers that lead to poor decisions, you can take proactive steps to avoid repeating past mistakes.

Spend time in prayer, asking God for wisdom and discernment in your decision-making. Seek His guidance in recognizing the triggers that lead to poor decisions and in developing habits that align with His will. Trust that God will provide the strength and clarity you need to make choices that reflect His love and lead to a more fulfilling and purposeful life.

Challenge Questions

1.   How can you recognize and manage the emotional states that lead to poor decision-making in your life? Consider developing practices such as mindfulness, prayer, and reflection to increase your awareness of your emotional triggers and responses.

2.   What steps can you take to seek God's wisdom and guidance when faced with difficult decisions? Make it a priority to spend time in God's Word, seek counsel from trusted mentors, and pray for His guidance and direction.

3.   Reflect on a decision you made in the past that was influenced by fear, boredom, hurt, or fatigue. What did you learn from that experience, and how can you apply those lessons moving forward? Use your past experiences as learning opportunities to grow in wisdom and resilience, trusting God to guide you on the path He has prepared.

By understanding the factors that contribute to poor decisions and seeking God's wisdom, we can make choices that reflect His love and lead to a more fulfilling and purposeful life. Embrace the opportunity to learn and grow, trusting that God will guide you on the path He has prepared.

Making wise decisions requires intentionality, self-awareness, and reliance on God's wisdom and strength. By recognizing the emotional triggers that lead to poor choices and seeking God's guidance, we can navigate life's challenges with confidence and grace. Trust that God is with you every step of the way, providing the wisdom and clarity you need to make choices that honor Him and fulfill His purposes for your life. Embrace the journey of growth and transformation, knowing that God will use every decision, both good and bad, to shape you into the person He created you to be.

Day 26:

Happiness vs. Marriage

Marriage is often portrayed as the ultimate source of happiness and fulfillment, a relationship where we find our "happily ever after." However, God did not call us to be happy in our marriages in the way the world often defines happiness. While God desires joy for us, the purpose of marriage goes far beyond personal satisfaction. Marriage is a covenant relationship through which God fulfills His greater purposes in our lives.

Understanding God's Purpose for Marriage

Marriage is not solely about personal happiness or the fulfillment of romantic ideals. It is a sacred covenant designed by God to accomplish His purposes in our lives and in the world. The Bible teaches that marriage is a divine institution that reflects God's love and serves as a partnership in fulfilling His plans.

Genesis 2:24 (NIV) provides the foundation for marriage: "That is why a man leaves his father and mother and is united to his wife, and they become one flesh."

This union is not just about happiness but about becoming one in purpose, mission, and growth. Together, you can accomplish things that neither of you could achieve alone. God brings two people together with unique gifts, strengths, and weaknesses, creating a partnership that can impact the world for His glory.

Marriage is a journey of mutual growth and transformation, where both partners are shaped and molded by God to become more like Christ. It is an opportunity to learn selflessness, patience, forgiveness, and unconditional love—qualities that are essential for reflecting God's character.

Embracing Triggers as Opportunities for Growth

In marriage, God uses your spouse to trigger things in you so that you can see what's on the inside, establish order, and receive healing. These triggers are opportunities to confront and address the hidden issues and emotions within you, leading to greater self-awareness and spiritual growth.

When conflicts arise or when your spouse's actions irritate you, it is easy to blame them and focus on their shortcomings. However, these moments are often opportunities for introspection and growth. Instead of blaming your spouse when you are triggered, stop and seek the Lord for your emotions. Allow His healing to transform your response and your heart.

Proverbs 27:17 (NIV) reminds us, "As iron sharpens iron, so one person sharpens another."

Marriage is a refining process where both partners are shaped and molded by God. By embracing this process, you can grow closer to each other and to God. Recognizing that your spouse is not your enemy but a partner in growth can help you navigate challenges with grace and understanding.

Working on Ourselves, Not Each Other

The media and Hollywood have distorted the example of marriage, making it look as though we are always happy or that we should leave when things get tough. However, the true path to a fulfilling marriage is through personal growth and transformation.

Rather than striving to change one another, focus on working on yourself. By addressing your own issues and seeking God's healing, you contribute to a healthier and more harmonious relationship. It is essential to recognize that you cannot change your spouse, but you can change your attitude, responses, and actions.

Matthew 7:3-5 (NIV) encourages self-reflection: "Why do you look at the speck of sawdust in your brother's eye and pay no attention to the plank in your own eye? How can you say to your brother, 'Let me take the speck out of your eye,' when all the time there is a plank in your own eye?"

By focusing on your own growth and allowing God to transform your heart, you set a positive example for your spouse and create an environment where both partners can thrive.

Breaking the Cycle of Dysfunction

If we do not work on ourselves and place blame on one another, we risk carrying our dysfunctions and issues into the next relationship, perpetuating a cycle of dysfunction. This is why many people marry over and over without finding true fulfillment.

Romans 12:2 (NIV) calls us to transformation: "Do not conform to the pattern of this world, but be transformed by the renewing of your mind."

By allowing God to transform our minds and hearts, we break free from the cycle of dysfunction and step into the fullness of His plans for our lives and marriages. Transformation begins with a willingness to confront our weaknesses, seek God's healing, and pursue growth and maturity.

Breaking the cycle of dysfunction requires a commitment to honesty, vulnerability, and accountability. It means being willing to confront brutal truths about ourselves and our relationship patterns and seeking God's grace to change and grow.

Finding Joy in God's Purpose

While marriage is not solely about happiness, it is designed to bring joy and fulfillment through the pursuit of God's purposes. By aligning our desires with God's will and embracing the transformative process of marriage, we can experience a more profound, more lasting joy that transcends temporary happiness.

Philippians 2:2 (NIV) urges us to "make my joy complete by being like-minded, having the same love, being one in spirit and of one mind."

True joy in marriage comes from unity of purpose, mutual love and respect, and a shared commitment to God's kingdom. As you work together to fulfill God's calling, you will discover the joy of being part of something more significant than yourselves.

Application

Reflect on your marriage or relationships and consider areas where you may have focused on happiness over growth. How can you embrace the refining process and seek God's purpose for your marriage?

Spend time in prayer, asking God to reveal areas in your heart that need healing and transformation. Seek His guidance in becoming the partner He has called you to be, committed to His purpose for your relationship.

Challenge Questions

1. How can you shift your perspective from seeking happiness in your marriage to embracing God's purpose and growth? Consider focusing on the qualities and virtues that God wants to develop in you and your spouse through your relationship.

2. In what ways can you allow God to use your marriage as a tool for healing and transformation? Reflect on the triggers and challenges in your marriage and invite God to use them as opportunities for growth and deeper intimacy.

3. Reflect on a time when you were triggered in your marriage. How can you respond with grace and seek God's guidance in your emotions? Practice patience and self-reflection, and seek God's wisdom in responding to challenges with love and understanding.

By understanding and embracing the true purpose of marriage, we can experience a deeper, more fulfilling relationship that reflects God's love and accomplishes His plans. Focus on growth, healing, and transformation, trusting that God will lead you on a path of true joy and fulfillment. Marriage is a sacred journey that offers endless opportunities for growth, partnership, and the realization of God's purposes in our lives.

Embrace the calling to be a partner in God's work, trusting that through His grace, your marriage will become a source of strength, joy, and testimony to His love. Allow God to shape and mold you through the challenges and joys of marriage, becoming more like Christ and reflecting His love to the world.

Day 27:

Courage is Greater than Strength

In the journey of life, we often seek strength to overcome the challenges and adversities we face. However, the Bible teaches us that courage is more essential than strength alone. Nearly every time Scripture encourages us to "be strong," it follows up with "and take courage." This pairing highlights a profound truth: strength without courage is useless. It is courage, grounded in trust in God, that empowers us to move forward and achieve great things.

Strength Without Courage

Strength alone cannot conquer fear. Even the most vital individuals can become paralyzed by fear and doubt. Strength without courage is like a car without gas—powerful in potential but unable to move forward. When fear grips our hearts, our physical or intellectual strength becomes ineffective.

Consider the Israelites standing at the edge of the Promised Land. Despite their numbers and potential, fear and a lack of courage prevented them from entering the land God had promised. In Numbers 13-14, we see that the spies sent to survey the land were intimidated by the giants and fortified cities. Their report spread fear among the Israelites, causing them to rebel against God's command to take the land. This story illustrates how strength, without courage, can lead to missed opportunities and prolonged struggles.

The Israelites' fear and reluctance to trust in God's promise resulted in wandering the wilderness for forty years. They had the strength in numbers and the backing of God's covenant, yet without courage, they faltered at the threshold of their destiny.

The Power of Courage

Conversely, courage built on trust in God can transform even the weakest into mighty warriors. Courage allows us to act despite fear, trusting in God's power and promises. One of the most potent examples of this is the story of David and Goliath.

David, a young shepherd boy armed with only a sling and a stone, faced the giant warrior Goliath. While others saw the giant's strength, David's courage, rooted in his trust in God, enabled him to see victory.

1 Samuel 17:45 (NIV) captures David's declaration: "David said to the Philistine, 'You come against me with sword and spear and javelin, but I come against you in the name of the Lord Almighty, the God of the armies of Israel, whom you have defied.'"

David's courage, founded on his faith in God, allowed him to defeat Goliath and secure victory for Israel. This story reminds us that when we trust in God, our courage can lead us to triumph over seemingly insurmountable challenges.

Courage and God's Promises

The Bible is filled with promises of God's presence and strength, which serve as the foundation for our courage. When we place our hope and trust in the Lord, we can face any challenge with confidence.

Psalm 31:24 (NIV) encourages us, "Be strong and courageous, all you who hope in the Lord."

Our strength and courage are not self-generated but are found in our relationship with God. By hoping in Him, we draw from His infinite power and love, empowering us to overcome obstacles and fulfill His purposes for our lives.

In **Joshua 1:9 (NIV)**, God commands Joshua, "Have I not commanded you? Be strong and courageous. Do not be afraid; do not be discouraged, for the Lord your God will be with you wherever you go." This assurance of God's presence provided Joshua with the courage to lead the Israelites into the Promised Land despite the formidable challenges ahead.

Be Encouraged

Whatever you're going through today, be encouraged because God is able to do it, and so are you. Here are a few ways to cultivate courage in your life:

1. **Seek God's Presence:** Spend time in prayer and worship, inviting God to strengthen your heart and fill you with His peace and

courage. Acknowledge His sovereignty over your situation and trust in His perfect plan.

2.   **Meditate on Scripture:** Reflect on Bible verses that speak of God's promises and faithfulness. Allow His Word to renew your mind and build your faith, providing a foundation for courage. **Psalm 119:105 (NIV)** declares, "Your word is a lamp for my feet, a light on my path." Let God's Word illuminate your path and guide your steps.

3.   **Remember Past Victories:** Recall times when God has been faithful in your life. Reflecting on past victories can inspire confidence and remind you of His ability to deliver you from current challenges. **1 Samuel 7:12 (NIV)** says, "Then Samuel took a stone and set it up between Mizpah and Shen. He named it Ebenezer, saying, 'Thus far the Lord has helped us.'" Remember your "Ebenezers," the moments when God's faithfulness was evident.

4.   **Take Action in Faith:** Courage is not the absence of fear but the willingness to act despite it. Step out in faith, trusting that God will guide and empower you as you move forward. **Hebrews 11:1 (NIV)** reminds us, "Now faith is confidence in what we hope for and assurance about what we do not see." Act on your faith, even when the outcome is uncertain.

Challenge Questions

1. In what areas of your life do you need to pair strength with courage to overcome challenges and pursue your calling? Consider how you can step out of your comfort zone and take bold steps of faith in those areas.

2. How can you cultivate a deeper trust in God's promises, allowing His strength and courage to guide your actions? Reflect on ways to deepen your relationship with God and strengthen your reliance on His Word.

3. Reflect on a time when God's presence gave you the courage to face a difficult situation. How can that experience inspire you to trust Him in your current circumstances? Use your past experiences as a source of encouragement and testimony to God's faithfulness.

By embracing the combination of strength and courage, we can navigate life's challenges with confidence and faith. Trust in God's promises, draw strength from His presence, and step forward with courage, knowing that He is with you every step of the way. As you cultivate a courageous spirit rooted in faith, you will find that God's power is made perfect in your weakness, enabling you to accomplish what seemed impossible.

Embrace courage over mere strength, for it is through courage that God's power is most vividly displayed in our lives. Let your trust in Him propel you forward, breaking through barriers and stepping into the fullness of His promises.

Day 28:

Fulfilling the Measure: Living Within Your God-Given Boundaries

In our journey of faith, understanding the concept of "measure" is crucial for living a life that aligns with God's purpose for us. The Greek word "metron," translated as "measure," refers to the boundary, dimension, space, or place of our spiritual jurisdiction. It defines the areas where God has given us authority and grace to operate effectively. By recognizing and embracing our measure, we can fulfill the unique calling God has placed on our lives.

The Biblical Concept of Measure

Understanding Our Measure

Ephesians 4:7 (NIV) states, "But to each one of us, grace has been given as Christ apportioned it." This verse highlights that God has given every believer a specific measure of grace to fulfill their calling. Just as a ruler sets the boundary of a length, our measure defines the scope of our influence and responsibility.

The apostle Paul elaborates on this concept in 2 Corinthians 10:12-16 (NIV): "We do not dare to classify or compare ourselves with some who commend themselves. When they measure themselves by themselves and compare themselves with themselves, they are not wise. We, however, will not boast beyond proper limits but will confine our boasting to the sphere of service God himself has assigned to us, a sphere that also includes you."

Paul acknowledges that God assigns each of us a specific sphere of service, a measure that we are responsible for stewarding. By understanding our measure, we can avoid the pitfalls of comparison and competition, focusing instead on fulfilling our unique role in God's kingdom.

The Parable of the Talents

The parable of the talents in Matthew 25:14-30 illustrates the principle of measure. In this parable, a master entrusts his servants with different amounts of talents according to their abilities. Some receive five talents, others two, and another one. Each servant is expected to multiply what they have been given.

The parable teaches that God does not give everyone the same abilities or responsibilities, but He expects us to use what we have been given faithfully. Our measure may differ from others, but we are all called to multiply what we have received for God's glory.

The Allotment of Land to Israel's Tribes

In Joshua 12-19, we see how God allocated specific boundaries to the tribes of Israel. Each tribe received a portion of the Promised Land, but the amounts and locations varied. This allocation illustrates that God gives each of us different measures, and we are called to conquer, possess, and become fruitful in the inheritance we have received.

Embracing Your Measure

Operating Within Your Measure

In your measure, God has given you realms of authority and grace. This is not saving grace but enabling grace that empowers you to operate within the measure of the gift of God in your life. Ephesians 4:16 (NIV) states, "From him, the whole body, joined and held together by every supporting ligament, grows and builds itself up in love, as each part does its work."

The body of Christ grows to the fullness of its measure when every individual part functions properly. By understanding and embracing our measure, we contribute to the overall health and growth of the church.

The Joy of Being Yourself

The most significant days of your life will come when you stop trying to be everyone else and recognize that Christ gives you the grace to live within the measure of who you are. God desires for you to be happy and content in being yourself because nobody is better at being you than you.

Psalm 139:13-14 (NIV) beautifully captures this truth: "For you created my inmost being; you knit me together in my mother's womb. I praise you because I am fearfully and wonderfully made; your works are wonderful, I know that full well."

Embracing Possibilities Within Your Measure

Within your measure, all things are possible! Even Christ understood His measure. In John 12:20-28, Jesus faced the Greeks who were seeking Him, and He recognized that His hour had come. His measure was not to win the world directly but to die and become the Savior of the world. By embracing His measure, Jesus fulfilled His purpose and brought salvation to humanity.

Similarly, Paul stated in 2 Corinthians 10:13 (NIV), "We, however, will not boast beyond proper limits but will confine our boasting to the sphere of service God himself has assigned to us." Paul recognized that the Corinthian church was part of his measure, giving him authority and responsibility within that sphere.

Living Out Your Measure

Fighting the Giants

To possess your land, you must be willing to fight giants. Just as the Israelites faced giants in the Promised Land, we will encounter challenges and obstacles within our measure. But with God's enabling grace, we can overcome these obstacles and fulfill our calling.

Numbers 13:30 (NIV) records Caleb's declaration: "Then Caleb silenced the people before Moses and said, 'We should go up and take possession of the land, for we can certainly do it.'"

Caleb's confidence in God's promises reminds us that we can conquer the giants in our measure and possess the land God has given us.

The Work Behind the Promise

"If it's a land of milk, then it's a land of work." The fulfillment of God's promises requires diligence, perseverance, and faithfulness. While God's grace empowers us, we must also put in the effort to work the land and cultivate the fruit God has promised.

Proverbs 14:23 (NIV) affirms, "All hard work brings a profit, but mere talk leads only to poverty." By committing to the work required within our measure, we align ourselves with God's purposes and experience the blessings of His promises.

Prophecy and Potential

Prophecy reveals our potential, but it is not inevitable. It means that what God has spoken is possible, but we must partner with Him to bring it to fruition. Prophecy is an invitation to step into our measure with faith and obedience.

1 Timothy 1:18 (NIV) urges us, "Timothy, my son, I am giving you this command in keeping with the prophecies once made about you, so that by recalling them you may fight the battle well."

By embracing prophecy as a call to action, we can fulfill the measure of our calling and see God's promises come to pass.

Application

Reflect on your understanding of your God-given measure. Are you operating within your measure, or are you trying to step outside of it? Consider how you can embrace your unique calling and contribute to the body of Christ.

Spend time in prayer, asking God to reveal your measure and the specific areas where He has called you to serve. Seek His guidance in recognizing the boundaries and responsibilities He has entrusted to you.

Challenge Questions

1. How can you identify and embrace your God-given measure, avoiding the temptation to compare yourself to others?

2. In what ways can you cultivate a mindset of content-ment and joy in being who God created you to be?

3. Reflect on a time when you experienced God's enabling grace within your measure. How can you continue to rely on His grace in your current circumstances?

By understanding and embracing our measure, we align ourselves with God's purposes and become effective instruments of His grace and truth. Trust in God's wisdom and provision, and embrace the fullness of your calling within the measure He has given you.

Day 29:

Real Ministry vs. Postmodern Style

In an era where image, popularity, and outward success often dominate cultural narratives, the church is not immune to these influences. The temptation to focus on church growth, celebrity status, and branding can overshadow the true essence of ministry. However, real ministry is about nurturing spiritual health, fostering genuine relationships, and cultivating Godly character. By focusing on these core values, we can align our efforts with God's purposes and reflect His love and truth to the world.

Church Health Over Church Growth

While numerical growth is often seen as a measure of success, faithful ministry prioritizes the health and spiritual vitality of the congregation. Healthy churches create an environment where believers can grow in their faith, develop strong relationships, and engage in meaningful service.

The focus on church health involves nurturing the spiritual well-being of the congregation, ensuring that individuals are grounded in their faith and equipped to live out their beliefs in their daily lives. Church health is about fostering a culture of discipleship, accountability, and spiritual growth.

Ephesians 4:15-16 (NIV) emphasizes the importance of maturity and unity: "Instead, speaking the truth in love, we will grow to become in every respect the mature body of him who is the head, that is, Christ. From him, the whole body joined and held together by every supporting ligament, grows and builds itself up in love, as each part does its work."

This passage highlights the importance of building a church community that grows in love and maturity rather than simply increasing in numbers.

Local Ministry Over Christian Celebrity

Real ministry focuses on serving the local community and meeting the needs of those around us. It is not about gaining fame or recognition but about embodying Christ's love and compassion in tangible ways. Local ministry involves engaging with the community, building relationships, and addressing the unique needs and challenges faced by those in our immediate surroundings.

Jesus modeled this approach, spending time with the marginalized, healing the sick, and teaching the lost. His ministry was rooted in personal relationships and local impact rather than seeking the spotlight.

John 13:34-35 (NIV) says, "A new command I give you: Love one another. As I have loved you, so you must love one another. By this, everyone will know that you are my disciples if you love one another."

Our love and service to our community are the hallmarks of true ministry, demonstrating the love of Christ in practical ways.

Godly Character Over Mad Skills

In a world that often values talent and charisma, Godly character is the foundation of authentic ministry. Skills and abilities can be impressive, but they mean little without integrity, humility, and a heart devoted to God.

Godly character involves living out the values of the Gospel in every aspect of our lives. It means prioritizing integrity, honesty, and compassion over personal gain or recognition.

1 Timothy 4:12 (NIV) encourages believers to lead by example: "Don't let anyone look down on you because you are young, but set an example for the believers in speech, in conduct, in love, in faith, and in purity."

Our character speaks louder than our abilities, reflecting the heart of Christ to those around us.

Personal Touch Over Mega Reach

While reaching a large audience can be impactful, faithful ministry emphasizes the value of personal connections. Jesus took time to engage with individuals, listen to their stories, and meet their needs. Building genuine relationships allows us to share God's love in a meaningful and lasting way.

The personal touch of ministry involves taking the time to invest in individuals, understanding their unique circumstances, and walking alongside them in their journey of faith. It is about being present and available, offering support and encouragement in a way that reflects the love of Christ.

Matthew 18:20 (NIV) reminds us, "For where two or three gather in my name, there am I with them."

Jesus valued intimate gatherings and personal interactions, demonstrating that true impact comes from meaningful relationships.

Pastor's Heart Over Ministry Brand

A pastor's heart is focused on shepherding the flock, providing care, guidance, and spiritual nourishment. This contrasts with a focus on building a ministry brand, which can lead to a focus on image and popularity rather than the well-being of the congregation.

Pastoral ministry involves being attentive to the needs of the congregation, offering spiritual guidance, and nurturing their growth in faith. It is about being a servant leader, prioritizing the spiritual health of the church over personal recognition or success.

1 Peter 5:2-3 (NIV) exhorts pastors to shepherd their flocks with humility and dedication: "Be shepherds of God's flock that is under your care, watching over them—not because you must, but because you are willing, as God wants you to be; not pursuing dishonest gain, but eager to serve; not lording it over those entrusted to you, but being examples to the flock."

Strong Souls Over Filled Seats

True ministry prioritizes the spiritual growth and strength of individuals over simply filling seats. Formed disciples are those who are grounded in God's Word, living out their faith and impacting the world for Christ.

The focus on forming disciples involves teaching, mentoring, and equipping believers to grow in their relationship with God and to live out their faith in practical ways. It is about helping individuals develop a deep and abiding belief that influences every aspect of their lives.

Colossians 1:28-29 (NIV) describes the goal of discipleship: "He is the one we proclaim, admonishing and teaching everyone with all wisdom, so that we may present everyone fully mature in Christ. To this end, I strenuously contend with all the energy Christ so powerfully works in me."

Discipleship involves a commitment to spiritual growth and maturity, leading to a deeper understanding of God's truth and a more significant impact on the world.

Love Over "Success"

In the end, love is the defining characteristic of real ministry. Success is not measured by numbers or recognition but by the depth of love and service demonstrated to others. Love involves selflessness, compassion, and a commitment to serving others in a way that reflects the heart of Christ.

1 Corinthians 13:1-3 (NIV) reminds us of the primacy of love: "If I speak in the tongues of men or of angels but do not have love, I am only a resounding gong or a clanging cymbal. If I have the gift of prophecy and can fathom all mysteries and all knowledge, and if I have a faith that can move mountains but do not have love, I am nothing."

Kind Over Cool, Humble Over Awesome

In a culture that often prioritizes being cool and awesome, genuine ministry values kindness and humility. Kindness involves treating others with compassion and respect, reflecting the love of Christ in every interaction.

Humility involves recognizing our dependence on God and placing others above ourselves. It is about serving others with a heart of gratitude and a desire to honor God in all that we do.

Philippians 2:3-4 (NIV) encourages us, "Do nothing out of selfish ambition or vain conceit. Rather, in humility, value others above yourselves, not looking to your own interests but each of you to the interests of the others."

Application

Reflect on your approach to ministry or your role within your church community. Are you prioritizing the values of real ministry over the allure of postmodern style? Consider how you can align your efforts with God's heart and purposes.

Challenge Questions

1.   How can you prioritize church health and personal relationships in your ministry or church community?

2.   In what ways can you cultivate Godly character and a servant's heart, focusing on love and service rather than recognition?

3.   Reflect on a time when you experienced the impact of real ministry in your life. How can you replicate that experience for others?

By focusing on the values of real ministry, we can create a community that reflects God's love, truth, and grace. Embrace the call to serve with humility, authenticity, and a heart devoted to God, trusting that He will use your efforts for His glory.

Day 30:

The Orphan Mindset

The orphan mindset is a pervasive issue affecting the spiritual and emotional lives of many people today. It causes individuals to strive for relevance, affirmation, acceptance, and accolades through their own efforts. This mindset compels them to scheme, lie, cheat, and steal to obtain these things, which may bring temporary benefits but ultimately cause harm in the long run. In contrast, true sons and daughters of God find their identity and security in Him, living in the fullness of their inheritance as beloved children of the Father.

Understanding the Orphan Mindset

The orphan mindset is characterized by a deep-seated sense of rejection, abandonment, and insecurity. It manifests as a constant need for approval and validation from others, leading to unhealthy behaviors and attitudes.

This mindset often results from experiences of rejection, trauma, or a lack of parental love and affirmation. Those affected by the orphan mindset feel disconnected from God and others, believing they must earn love and acceptance through their achievements and performance.

1.   Striving for Relevance and Acceptance

The orphan mindset drives individuals to strive for relevance and acceptance through worldly measures. They seek validation through success, accolades, and recognition, often compromising their values to gain approval.

Galatians 1:10 (NIV) warns against seeking human approval: "Am I now trying to win the approval of human beings, or of God? Or am I trying to please people? If I were still trying to please people, I would not be a servant of Christ."

This constant striving leads to exhaustion and dissatisfaction, as the orphan mindset can never be satisfied.

2. Manipulation and Deception

Those with an orphan mindset may resort to manipulation, deception, and dishonesty to gain acceptance and affirmation. These behaviors are driven by fear and insecurity, leading individuals to prioritize self-preservation over integrity and truth.

Proverbs 12:22 (NIV) reminds us, "The Lord detests lying lips, but he delights in people who are trustworthy."

These actions may provide temporary benefits, but they ultimately harm relationships and hinder spiritual growth.

Living as True Sons and Daughters

In contrast to the orphan mindset, true sons and daughters of God find their identity and security in their relationship with Him. They understand that their worth is not based on performance or achievements but on their status as beloved children of the Father.

1. Delighting in Living Hidden in the Beloved

True sons and daughters delight in living hidden in the Beloved, finding their rest and security in their relationship with God. They do not seek approval from the world but from their Heavenly Father, knowing that they are entirely accepted and loved by Him.

Colossians 3:3 (NIV) "For you died, and your life is now hidden with Christ in God."

This hiddenness provides a sense of peace and contentment, allowing believers to focus on their relationship with God rather than striving for worldly recognition.

2. Trusting in Father-Ordained Opportunities

True sons and daughters only take on opportunities marked with heaven's divine "Yes," trusting that God will provide the right opportunities at the right time. They do not chase after every opportunity but wait for those that align with God's will and purpose for their lives.

Proverbs 3:5-6 (NIV) encourages us, "Trust in the Lord with all your heart and lean not on your own understanding; in all your ways submit to him, and he will make your paths straight."

By trusting in God's timing and guidance, believers can focus on the "God thing" rather than simply pursuing "good things."

Embracing Our Identity in Christ

To overcome the orphan mindset and embrace our identity as true sons and daughters, we must recognize and accept the truth of who we are in Christ. This involves renewing our minds and rejecting the lies of the orphan mindset.

Romans 8:15-17 (NIV) reminds us of our identity as children of God: "The Spirit you received does not make you slaves so that you live in fear again; rather, the Spirit you received brought about your adoption to sonship. And by him, we cry, 'Abba, Father.' The Spirit himself testifies with our spirit that we are God's children. Now, if we are children, then we are heirs—heirs of God and co-heirs with Christ."

Steps to Embrace Our Identity

1. Renew Your Mind with God's Truth

Meditate on Scripture that affirms your identity as a beloved child of God. Allow His Word to transform your thinking and replace the lies of the orphan mindset with the truth of God's love and acceptance.

2. Cultivate Intimacy with the Father

Spend time in prayer and worship, seeking to deepen your relationship with God. Invite Him to reveal His heart for you and to strengthen your identity as His son or daughter.

3. Seek Healing and Restoration

If you have experienced rejection or trauma that has contributed to the orphan mindset, seek healing and restoration through counseling, prayer, and community support. Allow God to heal the wounds of the past and restore your identity as His beloved child.

4. Surround Yourself with Community

Engage with a community of believers who can support and encourage you in your journey of embracing your identity in Christ. Fellowship with others who understand their identity as sons and daughters can strengthen your faith and provide accountability.

Application

Reflect on areas in your life where the orphan mindset may be influencing your thoughts and behaviors. Consider how you can embrace your identity as a true son or daughter of God, finding security and acceptance in Him.

Spend time in prayer, asking God to reveal any areas where you are striving for approval and validation. Invite Him to renew your mind and strengthen your identity as His beloved child.

Challenge Questions

1. How can you recognize and reject the influence of the orphan mindset in your life, embracing your identity as a beloved child of God?

2. In what ways can you cultivate intimacy with the Father and trust in His timing and guidance for your life?

3. Reflect on a time when you experienced the love and acceptance of God as a true son or daughter. How can that experience inspire you to live in the fullness of your identity in Christ?

By embracing our identity as true sons and daughters, we can live in the freedom and fullness of God's love, reflecting His heart to the world. Trust in His promises, delight in His presence, and step confidently into the destiny He has prepared for you.

Day 31:

Stewarding God's Plan

In our spiritual journey, we may find ourselves in seasons where the clarity of God's calling becomes clouded by uncertainty and confusion. During these times, we can feel emotionally vulnerable, questioning the "why" and "how" of our circumstances. It is crucial to steward God's plan for our lives with wisdom and discernment, resisting the temptation to make impulsive decisions based on emotions or spiritual immaturity.

Navigating the Middle Season

When we encounter a middle season, where the initial excitement of our calling has waned, and the outcome remains unclear, it is easy to become discouraged. We may wonder if we misunderstood God's plan or if we should move on to something else. These feelings of vulnerability can lead us to make decisions that are not in alignment with God's purpose.

Resisting Impulsive Decisions

While God can release us and move us on from any situation, it is essential to ensure that it is indeed God leading us and not our emotional or spiritual immaturity. Impulsive decisions, driven by fear or frustration, can lead us away from God's path and cause us to forfeit the blessings He has in store.

Proverbs 19:21 (NIV) reminds us, "Many are the plans in a person's heart, but it is the Lord's purpose that prevails."

By remaining patient and seeking God's guidance, we can align our actions with His purposes and avoid unnecessary detours.

The Myth of Invulnerability

A common misconception is the belief that we are not powerful enough to mess up God's plans for our lives. While this idea may sound comforting, it is not entirely accurate. Our choices and actions can have significant consequences, and it is possible to forfeit God's best for us through disobedience or impatience.

The Importance of Stewardship

Stewarding God's plan requires intentionality and obedience. It involves being faithful to what God has entrusted to us, even when we don't understand the whole picture. By honoring our responsibilities and commitments, we demonstrate our trust in God's timing and wisdom.

Galatians 6:9 (NIV) encourages us, "Let us not become weary in doing good, for at the proper time we will reap a harvest if we do not give up."

Perseverance and faithfulness are essential qualities for stewarding God's plan and seeing His purposes fulfilled in our lives.

Remaining Faithful in Key Areas

To steward God's plan effectively, we must remain faithful in three key areas:

1. **Our Place** (Physical Location)

Our physical location is often integral to God's plan for our lives. He places us in specific environments and communities for a purpose. Moving prematurely, without God's direction, can disrupt the work He is doing in and through us.

Acts 17:26-27 (NIV) states, "From one man he made all the nations, that they should inhabit the whole earth; and he marked out their appointed times in history and the boundaries of their lands."

Trust that God has positioned you where you are for a reason, and seek His guidance before making any significant changes.

2. **Our People** (Covenant Relationships)

God places us in relationships that are vital for our growth and development. Covenant relationships, such as family, friendships, and spiritual community, provide support, accountability, and encouragement.

Hebrews 10:24-25 (NIV) exhorts us, "And let us consider how we may spur one another on toward love and good deeds, not giving up meeting together, as some are in the habit of doing, but encouraging one another—and all the more as you see the Day approaching."

Nurturing these relationships and remaining committed to the people God has placed in our lives is essential for stewarding His plan.

3. Our Process (Submission to the Work of the Holy Spirit)

God's plan often involves a process of refinement and growth. Submitting to the work of the Holy Spirit means allowing Him to shape and mold us, even when the process is uncomfortable or challenging.

Romans 8:28-29 (NIV) assures us, "And we know that in all things God works for the good of those who love him, who have been called according to his purpose. For those God foreknew, he was also predestined to conform to the image of his Son."

Trusting the process and remaining open to the Holy Spirit's leading allows us to grow in Christlikeness and fulfill our God-given purpose.

The Consequences of Jumping Ship

If we choose to abandon our place, people, or process prematurely, we risk forfeiting the blessings and opportunities God has prepared for us. While God's mercy can help us get back on track, there may be consequences to our choices.

The Fear of the Lord and Resilience

To steward God's plan effectively, we must cultivate a healthy fear of the Lord and resilience to persevere through challenges. The fear of the Lord involves reverence and awe for God's authority and wisdom, guiding us to make decisions that honor Him.

Proverbs 1:7 (NIV) declares, "The fear of the Lord is the beginning of knowledge, but fools despise wisdom and instruction."

Resilience, on the other hand, equips us to endure hardships and remain steadfast in our faith.

James 1:2-4 (NIV) encourages us, "Consider it pure joy, my brothers and sisters, whenever you face trials of many kinds, because you know that the testing of your faith produces perseverance. Let perseverance finish its work so that you may be mature and complete, not lacking anything."

Application

Reflect on the areas in your life where you may be tempted to make impulsive decisions based on emotions rather than God's guidance. How can you remain faithful in your place, people, and process, trusting in God's timing and wisdom?

Spend time in prayer, asking God to reveal any areas where you need to exercise patience and discernment. Invite Him to strengthen your resilience and deepen your fear of the Lord as you steward His plan for your life.

Challenge Questions

1. How can you ensure that your decisions are guided by God's wisdom rather than emotional or spiritual immaturity?

2. In what ways can you cultivate resilience and perseverance in your journey of faith, trusting in God's timing and purpose?

3. Reflect on a time when you remained faithful in a challenging season and saw God's purposes fulfilled. How can that experience inspire you to steward God's plan in your current circumstances?

By stewarding God's plan with faithfulness and discernment, we position ourselves to receive the blessings and fulfill the purposes He has prepared for us. Embrace the call to persevere, trusting that God is working all things for your good and His glory.

Day 32:

Biblical Illiteracy

How do you schedule your day for study, writing (journaling), and prayer? I understand that some of you may not be writers or care to write at all. But prayer and study are essential to your growth in Christ. The Bible is our spiritual nourishment, and prayer is our lifeline to God. If we neglect these practices, we starve our spirit and weaken our connection with the Lord.

2 Timothy 3:16-17: "All Scripture is God-breathed and is useful for teaching, rebuking, correcting and training in righteousness, so that the servant of God may be thoroughly equipped for every good work."

This scripture highlights the necessity of engaging with the Word of God daily. It's through Scripture that we receive the wisdom and training needed to live righteously and fulfill God's purpose for our lives.

The Problem of Biblical Illiteracy

Did you know that over 80% of the American church is considered to be Biblically illiterate? Most would not pass a Bible test given to 5th graders at a Christian school. This statistic is alarming because it means that the majority of believers lack a foundational understanding of God's Word. Without this foundation, how can we stand firm in our faith, make godly decisions, or share the gospel effectively?

Hosea 4:6: "My people are destroyed for lack of knowledge. Because you have rejected knowledge, I also reject you as my priests; because you have ignored the law of your God, I also will ignore your children."

The consequences of biblical illiteracy are severe. When we reject or neglect the knowledge of God, we open ourselves up to spiritual destruction. Ignorance of the Word leads to a weakened faith and vulnerability to deception.

The Impact of Increasing Biblical Literacy

If we were to somehow lower the percentage of biblical illiteracy, the results would be astonishingly excellent. There would be less counseling needed, more salvations, more giving, and therefore more income to strengthen churches to continue reaching even more people. A church that knows God's Word is a church that can effectively minister to others, grow in faith, and impact the world.

Joshua 1:8: "Keep this Book of the Law always on your lips; meditate on it day and night, so that you may be careful to do everything written in it. Then you will be prosperous and successful."

God's promise to Joshua applies to us as well. Meditating on God's Word and obeying it leads to prosperity and success—not just in material terms, but in spiritual growth and fruitful ministry.

Building a Culture of Study, Writing, and Prayer

The irony in this is that most of those reading this blog are not in the 80%. The fact that you are reading this means that you already have a desire to learn. So, to an extent, I'm once again preaching to the choir! But even among those who are dedicated to learning, there is always room for growth. Whatever you do, continue to build a culture of study, writing, and prayer every day.

Psalm 1:2: "But his delight is in the law of the Lord, and on his law, he meditates day and night."

Delighting in God's Word and meditating on it daily transforms our hearts and minds. It equips us to live according to God's will and to pass on what we learn to the next generation.

Application

Reflect on your daily habits of study, writing, and prayer. Are there areas where you can improve your consistency and depth? Consider setting aside dedicated time each day to engage with God's Word and to pray. If you haven't started journaling, try it out as a way to process what you're learning and to document your spiritual journey.

Spend time in prayer, asking God to increase your hunger for His Word and to give you wisdom as you study. Pray for the broader church, that biblical literacy would increase, and that believers would be equipped to fulfill their God-given purpose.

Challenge Questions

1. How can you create a more consistent routine for studying the Bible and praying each day?

2. In what ways can you encourage others in your church or community to prioritize biblical literacy?

3. Reflect on a time when your knowledge of Scripture helped you make a wise decision or minister to someone in need. How can you continue to grow in your understanding of God's Word?

By committing to study, prayer, and writing, we equip ourselves to live faithfully and to pass on the truths of God's Word to the next generation. Let's be a part of reversing the trend of biblical illiteracy, one day at a time.

Day 33:

Faith & Founding Fathers

I recently watched a documentary on the History Channel titled *The Secrets of Our Founding Fathers*. Its purpose is to allegedly expose the untold dark secrets of our nation's founders, questioning their intentions and motives. While it's true that our Founding Fathers were imperfect men, many of them were Bible-believing individuals of character and kingdom purpose. The documentary, like many revisionist efforts, attempts to cast doubt on the faith and values that played a crucial role in shaping our nation. This trend is part of a broader movement that seeks to undermine the influence of faith in America's history, a movement that the church must stand against.

The Faith of the Founding Fathers

Many of our Founding Fathers were deeply committed to their faith in Christ. They believed that faith was as important as education and freedom. For example, George Washington, the first President of the United States, often spoke of the importance of faith in public life. In his farewell address, Washington stated, "Of all the dispositions and habits which lead to political prosperity, religion and morality are indispensable supports." He recognized that without a moral foundation rooted in faith, the experiment of self-government would be in jeopardy.

Psalm 33:12: "Blessed is the nation whose God is the Lord, the people he chose for his inheritance."

Washington, along with many others, understood that the success of the new nation depended on its adherence to the principles of faith and morality. They saw the hand of God in the founding of America and believed that the nation's prosperity and freedom were gifts from God, contingent on the people's faithfulness to Him.

The Rise of Secularism and Revisionist History

Despite the strong faith of our Founding Fathers, our nation continues to spiral down into a secular society. The revisionist historical movement, which seeks to reinterpret and often distort history, is on the rise. These "historians" ignore and distort the faith of our Founding Fathers, presenting them as secularists or deists who did not value religious faith. This revisionism is not just an academic exercise; it is part of a broader effort to remove the influence of faith from public life.

Proverbs 14:34: "Righteousness exalts a nation, but sin condemns any people."

As the secular movement gains momentum, it seeks to abandon faith entirely. This is evident in the growing efforts to remove references to God from public spaces, to secularize education, and to marginalize those who hold to traditional religious beliefs. The revisionist historians and their allies in government and media are working to create a narrative that America was not founded on Christian principles, but rather on secular ideals.

The Church's Response

In response to these challenges, the church must stand firm and steadfast on its foundation of faith. We must understand that faith will never be purely logical or illogical; instead, it is theological. Faith does not ignore reality or knowledge; it adds God to the equation. Our faith is not mindless ignorance, nor is it limited by logical restraints. Instead, it is the founding cornerstone of our nation, encapsulated in the phrase "One nation under God."

Hebrews 11:1: "Now faith is confidence in what we hope for and assurance about what we do not see."

Faith is the lens through which we view the world, and it is the foundation upon which we build our lives and our society. As the secular movement seeks to remove faith from public life, the church must respond by returning to the basics of our faith: prayer and intercession, evangelism, and discipleship. These are the tools that God has given us to combat the forces of darkness and to bring about His kingdom on earth.

The Power of Prayer and Humility

At the end of the day, faith will be the difference-maker in the battle for the soul of our nation. Our solution has always been within our responsibility. God spoke it to Solomon at the dedication of the temple, providing a challenge and a promise. If executed, success, peace, and prosperity will always be the consequence.

2 Chronicles 7:14: "If my people, who are called by my name, will humble themselves and pray and seek my face and turn from their wicked ways, then I will hear from heaven, and I will forgive their sin and will heal their land."

This scripture is a call to action for believers. It reminds us that the future of our nation depends on our willingness to humble ourselves, pray, and seek God's face. When we turn from our wicked ways and seek God's forgiveness, He promises to heal our land. This is not just a promise for ancient Israel; it is a promise for every generation that seeks to follow God.

Application

Reflect on the current state of our nation and the role that faith plays in your life and in the lives of those around you. How can you stand firm in your faith in the face of growing secularism? Consider how you can be a light in your community, sharing the truth of God's Word and the importance of faith in public life.

Spend time in prayer, asking God to strengthen your faith and give you the courage to stand up for the truth. Pray for our nation, that God would heal our land, and that the principles of faith and morality would once again be honored.

Challenge Questions

1.   How can you actively combat the growing secularism in our society and promote the importance of faith in public life?

2.   In what ways can you return to the basics of faith, such as prayer, intercession, evangelism, and discipleship, in your own life?

3.   Reflect on the role of faith in the founding of our nation. How can you educate others about the true history of our Founding Fathers and the importance of faith in shaping our country?

By standing firm in our faith and returning to the foundational principles of prayer and humility, we can be a force for change in our nation. Let's take up the challenge to live out our faith boldly and to pass on the truth of God's Word to future generations.

Day 34:

Circumcision: The Journey of Spiritual Submission and Growth

"Paul wanted to take him along on the journey, so he circumcised him because of the Jews who lived in that area, for they all knew that his father was a Greek." (Acts 16:3)

Every time I read this passage, I can't help but think, "Ouch!" The act of circumcision, particularly in the context of an adult like Timothy, seems intense and painful. However, what stands out even more is Timothy's bravery and his unwavering commitment to the cause of Christ. These early believers were so Kingdom-focused that such significant and personal sacrifices were not even questioned. This passage is a powerful testament to the level of dedication required to fulfill God's purpose.

The First Lesson: Physical Circumcision as a Kingdom Strategy

Paul had a clear sense of mission when he decided to take Timothy under his wing. He knew that for Timothy to be effective in their ministry, particularly among the Jews, specific cultural barriers needed to be addressed. The Jews in the region knew that Timothy's father was Greek, and this could have posed a significant obstacle to their ministry efforts. Without circumcision, Timothy would have lacked the necessary credibility and voice among the Jewish people.

1 Corinthians 9:20: "To the Jews I became like a Jew, to win the Jews. To those under the law, I became like one under the law (though I myself am not under the law) so as to win those under the law."

Paul's decision to circumcise Timothy wasn't about legalism or adhering to old customs for their own sake. It was a strategic move to remove any hindrance that could prevent the Gospel from being heard. Timothy's willingness to undergo this procedure highlights his deep commitment to the mission and his readiness to do whatever it took to reach others for Christ.

The Second Lesson: A Life-long Spiritual Circumcision

Physical circumcision was just the beginning of Timothy's journey under Paul's mentorship. The more profound and ongoing circumcision was the circumcision of the heart and mind—a continual process of spiritual growth and character development. This was where true discipleship took place, a process that was likely painful at times and certainly challenging.

Romans 2:29: "No, a person is a Jew who is one inwardly; and circumcision is circumcision of the heart, by the Spirit, not by the written code. Such a person's praise is not from other people but from God."

Spiritual circumcision involves cutting away the attitudes and behaviors of the flesh that hinder our spiritual growth. This process is often facilitated by those we submit to spiritually—mentors, pastors, and spiritual fathers or mothers. Paul's role in Timothy's life wasn't just to guide him in ministry but to help him become a man of God, fully equipped to carry out the work of the Kingdom.

The Pain of Spiritual Circumcision: Offense and Growth

True apostolic discipleship often involves offense—not in the sense of harm or insult, but in the sense of challenging our comfort zones and confronting the areas of our lives that need to be refined. This process can be embarrassing, painful, and even frustrating at times. However, it is through these experiences that our character is shaped, and our spiritual maturity is developed.

Hebrews 12:11: "No discipline seems pleasant at the time, but painful. Later on, however, it produces a harvest of righteousness and peace for those who have been trained by it."

Just as physical circumcision was a sign of covenant and commitment in the Old Testament, spiritual circumcision is a sign of our covenant relationship with God. It is a commitment to allow God to cut away anything in our lives that does not align with His will. This process is essential for our growth and effectiveness in the Kingdom of God.

The Secret to Spiritual Circumcision: Staying Still and Trusting

One of the most challenging aspects of spiritual circumcision is the need to stay still and allow the process to happen. When we are being spiritually "cut on," the natural tendency is to want to run away, to justify quitting, or to resist the process. However, the key to successful spiritual circumcision is trust—trust in God, trust in the process, and trust in the people God has placed in our lives to help guide us.

Psalm 46:10: "He says, 'Be still, and know that I am God; I will be exalted among the nations, I will be exalted in the earth.'"

Staying still in the midst of correction, refinement, and growth is not easy, but it is necessary. It is in these moments of stillness and submission that God does His most profound work in us, preparing us for the greater purposes He has in store.

Application

Reflect on areas in your life where God may be calling you to submit to spiritual circumcision. Are there attitudes, behaviors, or mindsets that need to be cut away for you to grow and fulfill your purpose? Consider how you can trust God more fully in the process of spiritual refinement, even when it is uncomfortable or painful.

Spend time in prayer, asking God to reveal the areas of your heart and mind that need to be circumcised. Seek His strength to remain still and trust the process, knowing that He is preparing you for more incredible things.

Challenge Questions

1.   How can you embrace the process of spiritual circumcision in your life, even when it is challenging or uncomfortable?

2.   In what ways can you submit more fully to the spiritual authorities God has placed in your life, allowing them to guide and refine you?

3.   Reflect on a time when you resisted spiritual correction or growth. What did you learn from that experience, and how can you apply those lessons moving forward?

By allowing God to continually circumcise our hearts and minds, we position ourselves to be vessels of honor, fully equipped to carry out His will and purpose. Embrace the process, trust in His guidance, and stay still in His presence as He shapes you into the person He has called you to be.

Day 35:

The Breaking Point

"Peter replied, "Man, I don't know what you're talking about!" Just as he was speaking, the rooster crowed. The Lord turned and looked straight at Peter. Then Peter remembered the word the Lord had spoken to him: "Before the rooster crows today, you will disown me three times." And he went outside and wept bitterly." (Luke 22:60-62)

Much is said about the disciple Peter, whose role in the early church was paramount. The Peter we encounter in the Gospels is often impulsive, passionate, and sometimes brash. However, the Peter who emerges in the book of Acts is markedly different—steady, courageous, and a pillar of the early Christian movement. What happened to this man? While it is clear that the baptism of the Holy Spirit empowered him for ministry, there is another, more profound change that took place in his life—a transformation of character. This transformation often occurs when we reach a breaking point, a moment of profound realization and surrender.

We all have a breaking point. For Peter, this came with his denial of Christ. To fully grasp the significance of this moment, we must understand Peter's situation. He was a born leader, a successful entrepreneur, and someone who had given up everything to follow Christ. He had walked on water, been given the keys to the kingdom of God by Jesus, and even bravely cut off the ear of a soldier who came to arrest Jesus. Despite all these remarkable experiences, Peter had not yet encountered an actual breaking point—an experience that would strip away his self-reliance and expose the actual state of his heart.

Following Christ at a Distance

When the pressure was on, and the persecution became intense, Peter's true colors began to show. Luke 22:54 notes that Peter began to follow Christ at a distance: "Then seizing him, they led him away and took him into the house of the high priest. Peter followed at a distance." This detail is significant because it reveals the beginning of Peter's retreat into self-preservation. Following Christ from a distance symbolizes a shift from bold commitment to cautious hesitation, a move many of us make when faced with the fear of consequences.

We tend to distance ourselves from Christ when our hearts are more inclined toward self-preservation than toward standing firm in our faith. This is especially true in times of trial or when our faith is challenged by the world around us. For Peter, this distancing eventually led him to the courtyard where, by the warmth of a fire, he was cornered and confronted. Three times, he was asked if he was one of Jesus' disciples and three times, he denied knowing Christ. It was at that moment, just as the rooster crowed that Jesus turned and looked directly at Peter. The weight of his denial hit him like a wave, and he fled, weeping bitterly.

The Power of a Breaking Point

Breaking points are pivotal moments in our lives when God begins to cut away and break off the layers of residue caused by sin and self-reliance. These are often painful, humbling experiences, but they are necessary for our spiritual growth and for God to use us effectively. For Peter, his breaking point was essential to the development of his character. The impulsive, brash man we see in the Gospels became the humble, steadfast leader of the early church only after his heart was broken and remade by the Lord.

It was this breaking point that prepared Peter for his later ministry. The man who once denied Christ out of fear became the apostle who boldly preached to thousands at Pentecost, who stood firm before the Sanhedrin, and who ultimately gave his life for the sake of the Gospel. The transformation in Peter's character is evident not only in his actions but also in his writings. In his second epistle, Peter exhorts believers to make every effort to grow in their faith:

> *"For this very reason, make every effort to add to your faith goodness; and to goodness, knowledge; and to knowledge, self-control; and to self-control, perseverance; and to perseverance, godliness; and to godliness, brotherly kindness; and to brotherly kindness, love. For if you possess these qualities in increasing measure, they will keep you from being ineffective and unproductive in your knowledge of our Lord Jesus Christ. But if anyone does not have them, he is nearsighted and blind and has forgotten that he has been cleansed from his past sins." (2 Peter 1:5-9)*

These are the words of a man who understands the cost of discipleship and the importance of character. Peter's journey from impulsive disciple to steadfast apostle was not an easy one, but it was through his breaking point that he was refined and prepared for his ultimate purpose.

Application

Reflect on your own life and consider whether you have experienced a breaking point. Have you encountered moments where God has allowed you to face your limitations, your fears, or your failures? How did you respond? Breaking points are not meant to destroy us but to refine us. They are opportunities for God to strip away our self-reliance and rebuild us with a character that reflects Christ.

Spend time in prayer, asking God to reveal any areas in your life where you may be following Christ at a distance. Are there aspects of your faith where you are holding back out of fear or self-preservation? Invite the Holy Spirit to work in those areas, bringing about the transformation that only He can accomplish.

Challenge Questions

1. Have you experienced a breaking point in your spiritual journey? How did it change your character and your relationship with God?

2. In what ways might you be following Christ at a distance? What steps can you take to draw closer to Him, even in the face of fear or uncertainty?

3. How can you cultivate the qualities Peter describes in 2 Peter 1:5-9 in your own life? What practical steps can you take to add to your faith goodness, knowledge, self-control, perseverance, godliness, brotherly kindness, and love?

By embracing the breaking points in our lives, we allow God to refine our character, making us more effective for His kingdom. Like Peter, we can move from moments of failure to a life of faithful service, becoming the people God has called us to be.

Day 36:

Better Caught Than Taught

"I keep asking that the God of our Lord Jesus Christ, the glorious Father, may give you the Spirit of wisdom and revelation so that you may know him better. I pray also that the eyes of your heart may be enlightened in order that you may know the hope to which he has called you, the riches of his glorious inheritance in the saints, and his incomparably great power for us who believe..." (Ephesians 1:17-19)

Communicating the message of God can be challenging, especially when trying to convey the depth and nuance of what the Spirit is saying. As pastors and teachers of the Word, we often find ourselves burdened with the responsibility of ensuring that what we hear from God is clearly understood by those we minister to. This burden is not just about delivering a sermon but about truly imparting spiritual wisdom and revelation that can transform lives.

Preachers and teachers strive to improve their communication skills through various means—attending classes, participating in conferences, and even emulating great orators. However, despite our best efforts, there comes a point where human preparation meets the need for divine intervention. This is where the prayer of Paul in Ephesians becomes crucial. Paul understood that proper understanding and revelation come not just from human teaching but from the Spirit of God enlightening the hearts of the listeners.

The Role of the Spirit of Wisdom and Revelation

In Ephesians 1:17-19, Paul prays that God would give the Spirit of wisdom and revelation so that believers might know Him better. This prayer highlights a fundamental truth: spiritual understanding is a gift from God. It is not something that can be fully achieved through human effort alone. The Spirit of wisdom and revelation is essential for believers to grasp the deep things of God and to move beyond surface-level understanding to a more profound, more intimate knowledge of Him.

The "eyes of the heart" is a metaphor Paul uses to describe the inner person, the spiritual core that needs to be enlightened. Without this enlightenment, even the most eloquent and well-prepared sermons can fall flat. The message may

193

be heard with the ears, but it will not be "caught" by the heart. Spiritual truths, therefore, are often better caught than taught, requiring an openness to the Spirit's work in our lives.

The Burden of Communication

As ministers, we carry a burden for the people we serve. We long for them to understand and embrace the truths we are communicating. This burden can be heavy because we know that mere words are not enough. We can only do so much in our preparation and delivery. The rest is up to the Spirit of God to reveal and impress upon the hearts of the listeners.

This reality drives us to our knees in prayer, echoing Paul's request for the Spirit of wisdom and revelation. We must intercede for our congregations, asking God to open their spiritual eyes so they can truly grasp the hope of their calling, the richness of their inheritance in Christ, and the power available to them as believers.

The Power of Enlightenment

When the eyes of our hearts are enlightened, something miraculous happens. We move from merely hearing the Word to understanding and applying it in our lives. This enlightenment is not just intellectual but transformational. It affects how we see ourselves, how we see God, and how we live out our faith.

Paul's prayer in Ephesians is not just a prayer for knowledge but for experiential knowledge—a knowledge that comes from encountering God in a natural and personal way. This kind of knowledge changes us from the inside out. It moves us from being passive listeners to active participants in the work of the kingdom.

Application

As we seek to communicate God's Word effectively, we must recognize our dependence on the Spirit of God. Preparation is vital, but it must be coupled with prayer. We need to continually pray for the Spirit of wisdom and revelation, both for ourselves and for those we minister to. This prayer acknowledges that proper understanding and transformation come from God, not from our eloquence or expertise.

Reflect on your own approach to teaching and sharing the Word. Are you relying solely on your abilities, or are you actively seeking the Spirit's guidance and intervention? Make it a practice to pray for those you minister to, asking God to enlighten the eyes of their hearts so they may truly "catch" what the Spirit is saying.

Challenge Questions

1. **How often do you pray for the Spirit of wisdom and revelation before teaching or sharing the Word with others?** How can you incorporate this prayer more consistently into your preparation?

2. **In what ways have you seen the difference between something being "taught" and something being "caught" in your own spiritual journey?** How can this awareness shape your approach to learning and teaching?

3. **Reflect on a time when you experienced the "eyes of your heart" being enlightened.** What impact did it have on your understanding of God and His Word? How can you seek that kind of revelation more regularly in your life?

By embracing the reality that spiritual truths are often better caught than taught, we can align ourselves with the work of the Holy Spirit in our lives and in the lives of those we serve. As we pray for enlightenment, we open the door for deeper understanding, more significant transformation, and a more profound experience of God's presence and power.

Day 37:

The Art of Asking Questions

"Now the Berean Jews were of more noble character than those in Thessalonica, for they received the message with great eagerness and examined the Scriptures every day to see if what Paul said was true." (Acts 17:11)

This morning, as I was at Publix, a local grocery story, stocking up on some essentials, I encountered a situation that got me thinking deeply about how we approach learning and growth in our spiritual lives. As I was purchasing several large containers of water, I offered to the cashier that there were six of them, thinking she might use the quantity button to speed up the process. To my surprise, she laboriously scanned each one individually. Curiosity got the better of me, and I asked her why she didn't just use the quantity button. Her answer left me bewildered: "I don't ask any questions. I do what I'm told."

Her response made me reflect on how this mindset can often be found in the church as well. Too many believers follow spiritual instructions without asking why, without seeking deeper understanding, and without engaging their minds in the pursuit of truth. This kind of passive compliance leads to a shallow faith that lacks the robustness needed to withstand the challenges of life. In contrast, the Berean Jews mentioned in Acts 17:11 were commended for their eagerness to examine the Scriptures and verify the truth of what they were taught.

The Importance of Asking Questions

Asking questions is not just a sign of curiosity; it's a pathway to more profound knowledge and understanding. The process of asking questions helps us to engage more fully with the material we are learning, whether it's a sermon, a Bible study, or a personal reading of Scripture. It allows us to dig beneath the surface and discover the layers of meaning and application that God has for us.

When we ask questions, we demonstrate a desire to truly understand and internalize the truths we are encountering. Jesus Himself often asked questions to provoke thought and reflection in His listeners. For example, in Matthew 16:15, He asks His disciples, "But what about you? Who do you say I am?" This ques-

197

tion wasn't because Jesus didn't know the answer but because He wanted His disciples to think deeply about their own beliefs and understanding.

Ignorant Compliance vs. Ignorant Rebellion

In the church, we often see two extremes: those who follow without question (ignorant compliance) and those who rebel without understanding (ignorant rebellion). Both are problematic because they prevent growth and maturity in the faith.

Ignorant compliance is when believers accept everything they are taught without seeking to understand the reasoning or scriptural basis behind it. This can lead to a faith that is easily shaken when faced with challenges or when confronted with opposing viewpoints.

Ignorant rebellion, on the other hand, is when believers reject teachings or practices without fully understanding them or seeking God's guidance on the matter. This attitude can lead to a spirit of stubbornness and a refusal to grow or learn from others.

Both attitudes are dangerous because they close the door to growth. True spiritual maturity requires us to be both submissive to God's authority and inquisitive about His ways. We are called to be like the Bereans, who received the message with eagerness but also examined the Scriptures daily to see if what they were being taught was true.

The Benefits of Mastering the Art of Asking Questions

When we develop the habit of asking questions, we unlock new levels of understanding and wisdom. This practice is critical in our study of Scripture. As we read, we should be asking questions like:

- What does this passage mean?

- How does this apply to my life?

- What is God trying to teach me through this?

- How does this connect to other Scriptures I've read?

By asking these kinds of questions, we allow the Holy Spirit to guide us into more profound truth and understanding. It also equips us to better share our faith with others, as we become more knowledgeable and confident in what we believe.

Application

As you go about your day, make it a habit to ask questions—whether in your study of the Word, in conversations with others, or in your everyday experiences. Don't be afraid to seek out answers and engage in discussions that challenge and stretch your understanding. Remember, growth comes not from passively accepting what we are told but from actively seeking to understand and apply it.

When you study Scripture, approach it with a questioning mind. Ask God to open your eyes and give you understanding. Be like the Bereans who examined the Scriptures daily, eager to understand and apply God's truth.

Challenge Questions

1.   How often do you ask questions when studying the Bible? Reflect on your study habits and consider how you can incorporate more inquiry into your time in the Word.

2.   Have you ever found yourself in a place of ignorant compliance or rebellion? How did that impact your spiritual growth, and what steps can you take to move toward a more inquisitive and mature faith?

3.   Think of a recent sermon or teaching you heard. What questions did it raise for you? How can you seek out the answers to those questions this week?

By embracing the art of asking questions, we position ourselves to grow in wisdom and understanding, deepening our relationship with God and our ability to live out our faith with confidence and clarity.

Day 38:

Paul's Sermon Series: Embracing Hardships as a Pathway to the Kingdom

"They preached the good news in that city and won a large number of disciples. Then, they returned to Lystra, Iconium, and Antioch, strengthening the disciples and encouraging them to remain true to the faith. 'We must go through many hardships to enter the kingdom of God.'" (Acts 14:22)

The Apostle Paul's ministry was marked by incredible success and fruitfulness. He preached the gospel, won significant numbers of converts, and, more importantly, made disciples. His ministry was not just about conversions; it was about strengthening and encouraging believers to remain true to the faith. This season of Paul's ministry was undoubtedly productive, with much spiritual fruit being borne. It was a time of significant advancement for the kingdom of God. But was it all smooth sailing?

The Reality of Paul's Ministry: Success Through Suffering

In today's church, particularly in the Western context, success is often measured by the absence of difficulties and the presence of material prosperity. The modern church frequently equates a smooth, trouble-free life with God's favor and financial abundance with spiritual blessing. This mindset, however, is far removed from the ideology and experiences of the Apostle Paul.

Paul understood a critical principle that is often overlooked in contemporary Christianity: success and fruitfulness in ministry usually come through trials, hardships, and persecution. In Acts 14, while Paul was seeing great success in his ministry, he was also experiencing severe persecution. In fact, he was stoned and left for dead during this time. Despite this, Paul did not waver in his mission; he continued to preach the gospel and strengthen the disciples.

Paul's success was not in spite of his hardships but rather because of them. He knew that the afflictions he faced were the very means through which God was releasing His power and presence in and through him. This is what Paul

201

meant when he talked about "outer affliction—inner release." The pressure and persecution he faced externally were catalysts for the release of God's power internally.

A Sermon Series Unlike Any Other

Paul's ministry strategy during this season could be summarized in one sermon series: "We must go through many hardships to enter the kingdom of God." This was not a message designed to attract large crowds with promises of ease and prosperity. Instead, it was a message of reality, encouraging believers to understand that following Christ often involves suffering and sacrifice.

Paul's message was not just about enduring hardships but about understanding their purpose. He taught that trials, testing, and tribulations are not obstacles to avoid but opportunities to embrace. These challenges serve to strengthen our faith, refine our character, and deepen our dependence on God. They clear our minds of superficial concerns and focus our hearts on what truly matters.

The Modern Church's Misunderstanding of Success

Unfortunately, the modern church often shies away from this kind of message. Instead of preparing believers for the inevitable hardships of life, the church sometimes spends more time and resources trying to make the Christian life comfortable and convenient. We coddle and pamper believers, trying to keep them from quitting rather than equipping them to endure hardships and grow through them.

This approach, however well-intentioned, does a disservice to the body of Christ. Strength is not developed through ease and comfort but through resistance. Just as muscles grow stronger when they are challenged with weight and resistance, our faith grows more robust when it is tested through trials and tribulations.

When the church focuses too much on comfort and convenience, it risks creating a generation of believers who are weak in faith, easily distracted, and ill-prepared for the challenges of life. Paul understood this danger, which is why he was so committed to preaching a message that prepared believers for the reality of the Christian life.

The Strengthening Power of Trials

Paul's sermon series, "We must go through many hardships to enter the kingdom of God," was not just a warning; it was an invitation to grow stronger in the faith. Trials, testing, and tribulations are not meant to destroy us but to strengthen us. They force us to reassess our values, evaluate what is truly important, and focus on what really matters.

When we face hardships, we are stripped of superficial concerns and forced to confront the deeper issues of life. This process of refining is painful but necessary. It is through these challenges that God strengthens our faith, deepens our character, and prepares us for greater responsibilities in His kingdom.

Application

Reflect on your own life and ministry. How do you view trials and hardships? Do you see them as obstacles to be avoided or as opportunities for growth? Take time to reassess your values and evaluate what is truly important in your life. Consider how God might be using your current challenges to strengthen your faith and prepare you for more excellent service in His kingdom.

Spend time in prayer, asking God to help you embrace the hardships you face with faith and courage. Ask Him to show you how He is using these challenges to refine your character and deepen your dependence on Him.

Challenge Questions

1. How do you typically respond to trials and hardships in your life? Do you see them as opportunities for growth, or do you try to avoid them at all costs?

2. In what ways can you begin to view the difficulties you face as a means of spiritual growth and strengthening? How can you change your perspective to align more closely with Paul's teachings?

3. How can you encourage others in your community of faith to embrace hardships as a pathway to spiritual maturity? What practical steps can you take to help others grow through their trials?

By embracing the reality of trials and hardships, we can develop a deeper, stronger faith that is resilient and steadfast. Let us learn from Paul's example and allow God to use the challenges we face to shape us into vessels fit for His kingdom.

Day 39:

Outward Affliction...Inner Release

"Therefore we do not lose heart. Though outwardly, we are wasting away, inwardly, we are being renewed day by day. For our light and momentary troubles are achieving for us an eternal glory that far outweighs them all. So, we fix our eyes not on what is seen but on what is unseen. For what is seen is temporary, but what is unseen is eternal." (2 Corinthians 4:16-18)

Life often teaches us valuable lessons, sometimes through difficult circumstances. A few years ago, I learned a critical truth that has since transformed my outlook on life: "If I don't like what I'm getting in life, then I have to change what I'm doing." This realization came after I grew weary of living in cycles of diminished returns. I became determined to break those cycles and step into seasons of perpetual fruitfulness.

The key to this transformation was a deep and often painful process: I began to die to myself. I realized that outward battles, trials, and tribulations were not just random occurrences—they were designed to outwardly waste away the carnal aspects of my being. This wasn't just about the physical body but more about the soul—the mind, will, and emotions. Through this process, I learned several vital truths.

1. What I'm Going Through Is Temporary

"For our light and momentary troubles are achieving for us an eternal glory that far outweighs them all." (2 Corinthians 4:17)

The first thing I learned was that my afflictions, no matter how intense, were temporary. Paul refers to them as "light and momentary troubles." This perspective is crucial because it reminds us that our trials are not permanent fixtures in our lives. They are temporary phases that we pass through on our way to something greater. Understanding this helps us to endure hardships with hope, knowing that they are not the end of the story.

2.   Afflictions Have an Assignment

"For our light and momentary troubles are achieving for us an eternal glory that far outweighs them all." (2 Corinthians 4:17)

I realized that the trials I faced were not pointless; they had an assignment. Their purpose was to kill the self-centered, carnal aspects of my nature so that the life of Christ in me could come forth more fully. These outward afflictions were tools in the hands of God, used to refine my character and make me more like Christ. If I failed to respond to them instead and adequately became consumed by them, I would miss out on the eternal glory they were meant to produce in me.

3.   Affliction Prepares Us for Greater Glory

"For our light and momentary troubles are achieving for us an eternal glory that far outweighs them all." (2 Corinthians 4:17)

The weight of affliction I carry is not just a burden; it is also preparation. It is preparing me for a greater weight of glory that is coming. This is a profound truth that shifts our perspective on suffering. Rather than seeing affliction as something to avoid at all costs, we begin to see it as a necessary part of our spiritual journey. The trials we face today are building the capacity in us to carry the glory of God tomorrow.

4.   The Bridge from Glory to Glory Is Affliction

"We must go through many hardships to enter the kingdom of God." (Acts 14:22)

One of the most important lessons I learned is that the bridge that leads from one level of glory to the next is the bridge of affliction. God is always taking us from glory to glory, from faith to faith, and from strength to strength. But to move from one level to the next, we must pass through trials and tribulations. These experiences are not roadblocks but stepping stones on the path to greater spiritual maturity and fruitfulness.

5.   Fix Your Eyes on the Unseen

"So we fix our eyes not on what is seen, but on what is unseen. For what is seen is temporary, but what is unseen is eternal." (2 Corinthians 4:18)

Finally, I learned the importance of focus. In the midst of trials, it's easy to become fixated on the problems we see around us. But Paul reminds us to fix our eyes on what is unseen. This means focusing on the eternal truths and promises of God rather than the temporary circumstances we face. By keeping our focus on the unseen, we align ourselves with God's eternal purposes and find the strength to endure our current challenges.

Application

As you reflect on your own life, consider how you have responded to the trials and tribulations you've faced. Have you seen them as opportunities for growth and preparation, or have you become consumed by them? Take some time to meditate on the truths outlined above. Ask God to help you see your afflictions from His perspective and embrace the process of being renewed inwardly, even as you face outward challenges.

Spend time in prayer, asking God to help you fix your eyes on the unseen and to trust Him with the process of your spiritual growth. Ask Him to reveal the purpose behind your trials and to give you the strength to endure them with faith and perseverance.

Challenge Questions

1. How do you typically respond to trials and afflictions in your life? Do you see them as opportunities for growth, or do you try to avoid them at all costs?

2. In what ways can you begin to view your current challenges as part of God's preparation for greater glory? How can you change your perspective to align more closely with Paul's teachings?

3. What steps can you take to fix your eyes on the unseen and focus on God's eternal purposes rather than your temporary circumstances? How can you encourage others to do the same?

By embracing the process of outward affliction and inner renewal, we can grow in our faith and become vessels fit for God's glory. Let us learn to see our trials not as obstacles but as opportunities for God to do His transformative work in us.

Day 40:

Passion + Problems = Purpose

We were designed to solve problems. The things we use today, like doorknobs, glasses, chairs, shoes, microphones, etc., were all created to solve problems. A problem existed, and an invention was created.

In life, we often encounter problems that seem overwhelming or insurmountable. Yet, if we look closely, these very problems are the catalysts for creativity and innovation. Every invention we rely on today starts with a problem that needs solving. From the simplest tool to the most complex technology, issues have driven people to create, innovate, and bring new solutions into the world.

Problems as Catalysts for Creativity

Problems are not just obstacles; they are opportunities. They are the triggers that ignite creativity and innovation. Inventors, creators, and thinkers direct their passion toward these problems, and in doing so, they uncover solutions that not only resolve the issue at hand but also serve a greater purpose. Everything in life, from the most basic tools to the most advanced technologies, was created with a purpose—to solve a problem.

Everything in life has a purpose. And yes, even problems have a purpose. The purpose of problems is to build your passion in such a way that you pursue your purpose in order to solve the problem!

This perspective shifts how we view the challenges we face. Problems are not just inconveniences or hurdles; they are purposeful. They exist to stir up something within us, to push us toward our purpose. Without problems, we might never discover the depth of our passion or the true direction of our purpose.

The Relationship Between Passion and Problems

You were designed, intended, and purposed to solve problems. Problems will come, but will only leave when they are solved. Without passion, problems have permanent residency.

Problems are an inevitable part of life. They will always come, but they are not meant to stay. When a problem lingers, it often indicates a lack of passion to address and solve it. Passion is the fuel that drives us to confront problems head-on. It's what motivates us to find solutions, to push through obstacles, and to keep going even when the path is difficult.

We are all on a journey to discover purpose. However, the purpose will never be discovered outside of problems. And if we don't marry passion with our problems, we will never produce our purpose.

The journey to discovering our purpose is intertwined with the problems we face. Our purpose is often hidden within the problems that challenge us the most. But it's not just the problems themselves that lead us to our purpose; it's the passion we bring to solving them. When we approach problems with passion, we unlock the door to our purpose. Passion gives us the energy, creativity, and determination to overcome challenges and fulfill our God-given purpose.

The Necessity of Producing Your Purpose

It is very necessary for you to produce your purpose for the reason that you are the solution to someone else's problems. You are a walking solution to somebody. You are needed! You are necessary to someone!

Your purpose is not just about you; it's about the impact you have on others. You were created to be a solution to someone else's problem. Your life, your experiences, and your unique set of skills and passions are all part of a bigger plan. There are people in this world who need what you have to offer. When you fulfill your purpose, you become a blessing to others. You are not just living for yourself; you are living to make a difference in the lives of those around you.

Passion: The Key to Unlocking Purpose

Here's the clincher… Problems are produced automatically by life; they are a guaranteed entity. On the other hand, you must generate passion. So, it is safe to say that living among problems and not knowing the purpose is simply the absence of PASSION.

While problems are inevitable, passion is something we must cultivate. It doesn't come automatically; it requires intentionality. Passion is the driving force that compels us to confront problems and find solutions. Without passion, problems can overwhelm us, leaving us stuck and purposeless. But when we generate passion—through prayer, reflection, and a deep commitment to our values and beliefs—we can transform problems into opportunities to fulfill our purpose.

Application

As you reflect on the problems in your life, ask yourself where your passion lies. Are there challenges that you have been avoiding because they seem too difficult? Consider how you can approach these problems with a renewed sense of passion and purpose. Remember, you were designed to solve problems, and within those problems lies the key to your purpose.

Spend time in prayer, asking God to reveal the passions He has placed in your heart and how they align with the problems you are facing. Ask Him to give you the strength and determination to confront these challenges with faith and creativity. Trust that as you do so, you will discover the purpose He has for you.

Challenge Questions

1. What problems are you currently facing that could be opportunities for discovering your purpose? How can you shift your perspective to see these challenges as catalysts for growth and creativity?

2. In what areas of your life do you need to cultivate more passion to solve the problems you encounter? How can you intentionally generate passion in these areas?

3. Who in your life needs the solution that only you can provide? How can you begin to step into your purpose by addressing the needs of those around you?

By embracing the connection between passion, problems, and purpose, we can live lives of greater impact and fulfillment. Let's commit to solving the problems before us with passion, knowing that in doing so, we are fulfilling the purpose for which we were created.

Day 41:

Persecution vs. Unity

"Go stand in the temple courts and tell the people the full message of this new life" *(Acts 5:20).*

In the early days of the church, unity was the powerful force that enabled the disciples to achieve incredible feats. It wasn't just about gathering together; it was about moving in one accord, with one heart and one purpose. This unity brought with it a host of blessings: revival, power, momentum, boldness, focus, structure, order, government, creativity, and anointing. The early church in Jerusalem, as described in the Book of Acts, exemplified this kind of unity. But this unity wasn't easily attained—it was forged through the fires of persecution.

The Power of Unity

"When the day of Pentecost came, they were all together in one place" (Acts 2:1).

Unity is the bedrock of any powerful movement. When people come together with a shared purpose, their combined efforts create an environment where extraordinary things can happen. In Acts 2:1, the early believers were gathered together in one place, in one accord. This unity was the fertile ground that allowed the Holy Spirit to move mightily among them. As a result, revival broke out, and the church grew exponentially.

Corporate unity brings with it friends like revival, power, and boldness. When a group of people is united, they are able to pool their resources, talents, and anointing to achieve great things. Unity also brings focus, structure, and order, allowing the group to move forward with clarity and purpose. This was the experience of the Jerusalem church—they were able to operate in the fullness of God's power because they were united in their mission.

The Role of Persecution in Achieving Unity

"Then the high priest and all his associates, who were members of the party of the Sadducees, were filled with jealousy. They arrested the apostles and put them in the public jail" (Acts 5:17-18).

Persecution, often seen as a tool of the enemy to destroy the church, actually played a significant role in strengthening the unity of the early believers. Persecution has a way of stripping away superficial differences and forcing people to focus on what truly matters. When the apostles were arrested and thrown in jail, they were reminded of their dependence on God and on each other. Persecution reduces us to the lowest common denominator, reminding us that we are all in this together and that we all face a common threat.

This common threat brought the apostles closer together. Rather than allowing persecution to divide them, they allowed it to unify them even more. They realized that their survival and success depended on their ability to stand together in the face of adversity. In this way, persecution served as a catalyst for greater unity among the believers.

The Angel's Command: A Call to Unity

"But during the night an angel of the Lord opened the doors of the jail and brought them out. 'Go, stand in the temple courts,' he said, 'and tell the people all about this new life'" (Acts 5:19-20).

In the midst of persecution, God sent an angel to deliver the apostles from prison. The angel's command to them was simple: "Go, stand in the temple courts, and tell the people the full message of this new life." This was not just a command to preach the gospel; it was a call to stand together in unity and continue their mission despite the opposition they faced.

Persecution gave the apostles the strength to stand together. It stripped away any competition, prejudices, or offenses that might have existed among them. In standing together, they were able to pool their gifts, talents, and anointing to create a concerted effort to spread the gospel. They understood that no one was dispensable—when one hurt, all hurt. This deep sense of unity allowed them to face persecution with boldness and confidence, knowing that they were not alone in their struggle.

The Blessing of Persecution

"Consider it pure joy, my brothers and sisters, whenever you face trials of many kinds, because you know that the testing of your faith produces perseverance" (James 1:2-3).

Persecution, though painful, is a blessing in disguise. It is through persecution that our faith is tested, and our character is refined. It forces us to rely on God and on each other in ways that we might not otherwise. It is in the crucible of persecution that true unity is forged. The early church understood this, and they embraced persecution as a means of strengthening their resolve and deepening their unity.

Application

Reflect on your own life and the challenges you face. Are there areas where persecution or opposition is threatening to divide you from others? Consider how you can use these challenges as opportunities to deepen your unity with those around you. Instead of allowing difficulties to create division, use them to draw closer to God and to the people He has placed in your life.

Spend time in prayer, asking God to give you the strength and courage to stand together with others in the face of persecution. Ask Him to help you see the blessings that come from standing in unity and to give you the grace to remain true to the faith, even when times are tough.

Challenge Questions

1. How can you cultivate unity in your own life and within your community, especially in the face of persecution or opposition? What practical steps can you take to ensure that challenges bring you closer to others rather than driving you apart?

2. In what ways can persecution or trials in your life serve as a catalyst for deeper unity and greater strength? How can you shift your perspective to see these challenges as opportunities for growth rather than threats?

3. How can you support others who are facing persecution or challenging times? In what ways can you stand together with them, pooling your resources and gifts to create a more substantial, more unified effort in fulfilling God's mission?

By understanding the relationship between persecution and unity, we can embrace the challenges we face and use them as opportunities to grow closer to God and to each other. Let's commit to standing together in unity, no matter what opposition we face, knowing that God is with us and that He will use our unity to accomplish great things.

Day 42:

Thoughts on Unity & Teamwork

"How good and pleasant it is when God's people live together in unity!" (Psalm 133:1)

Unity is a non-negotiable component of any victorious team. A spirit of cooperation is the glue that holds a team together, allowing it to function as a single, cohesive unit. When team members are united in their goals and intentions, they are more likely to achieve success. Unity doesn't mean uniformity but rather a harmonious blend of diverse talents and perspectives working toward a common goal.

A unified team is one where each member understands their role and contributes to the collective effort without selfish ambition. This cooperation fosters an environment where everyone feels valued and essential to the team's success. When a team operates in unity, it moves with one heartbeat, one purpose, and one direction, leading to remarkable achievements.

The Willingness to Be Confronted

"Faithful are the wounds of a friend; profuse are the kisses of an enemy." (Proverbs 27:6)

For a team to thrive, there must be a willingness among its members to be confronted and to confront others in love. This principle was demonstrated when David's mighty men came to him while he was fleeing from Saul. David asked them, "Why did you come?" (1 Chronicles 12:17). Leaders should not hesitate to ask team members tough questions, like "Why are you here?" to ensure that everyone's motives align with the team's goals.

Confrontation, when done in love and with the right intentions, leads to growth and unity. It allows team members to address issues before they fester and cause division. A team that avoids necessary confrontation is a team that risks internal strife and misalignment. Therefore, the willingness to be confronted is essential for maintaining the health and integrity of the team.

Submission to Leadership and Each Other

"Again, truly I tell you that if two of you on earth agree about anything they ask for, it will be done for them by my Father in heaven." (Matthew 18:19)

Submission is often misunderstood, but it is a powerful principle in any successful team. It's not just about submitting to the leader; it's also about submitting to one another. In Matthew 18:19, the term "agree" is likened to a symphony where all parts work in harmony. The agreement is where God's power is most evident.

Submission fosters an environment where team members are willing to listen, learn, and grow from one another. It removes the barriers of pride and self-will, allowing the team to function smoothly and effectively. When team members submit to each other's strengths, the team becomes stronger and more resilient, able to tackle challenges with collective wisdom and grace.

Shared Vision and Values

"Where there is no vision, the people perish: but he that keepeth the law, happy is he." (Proverbs 29:18)

A shared vision is the driving force behind any successful team. Vision excites and unites people, giving them something to strive for together. However, vision alone is not enough; there must also be a shared system of values. Values guide how the team operates, helping to prioritize efforts and maintain consistency in decision-making.

Most conflicts within teams, particularly in churches, do not arise from differences in vision but from differences in values and philosophy. When values are not aligned, it becomes challenging to maintain unity and focus. Therefore, a team must regularly revisit and reinforce its shared vision and values to ensure everyone remains on the same page.

Combined Determination

"Therefore, my dear brothers and sisters, stand firm. Let nothing move you. Always give yourselves fully to the work of the Lord, because you know that your labor in the Lord is not in vain." (1 Corinthians 15:58)

Unity breeds determination. When a team operates in unity, its members become self-starters, motivated not by external rewards but by a shared commitment to the team's mission. They become "second-milers," willing to go above and beyond to achieve the team's goals.

Combined determination also multiplies the team's faith. When everyone is working together, believing in the same vision, the power of that collective faith can move mountains. In such an environment, challenges are met with a unified resolve, and obstacles are seen as opportunities to grow stronger.

Corporate Unity and Followership

"At once they left their nets and followed him." (Matthew 4:20)

In a team that values corporate unity, there is a natural desire to follow the leader and the collective mission. The disciples left everything to follow Jesus because they were united in their desire to be part of something greater than themselves. In the same way, a team united in purpose will willingly follow where the vision leads, knowing that they are contributing to a cause that matters.

The Desire to Be Shaped

"As iron sharpens iron, so one person sharpens another." (Proverbs 27:17)

Unity also brings a desire to be shaped. It is impossible to shape people who do not share the team's values and vision. Team members must be willing to be molded and refined, understanding that the process of shaping is essential for growth and effectiveness.

The Role of Relationships

"Two are better than one, because they have a good return for their labor: If either of them falls down, one can help the other up. But pity anyone who falls and has no one to help them up." (Ecclesiastes 4:9-10)

No one succeeds alone. Every leader needs relationships that strengthen and support them. Every Paul needs a Barnabas, who will partner with him and take him to another level. Every Paul needs a Silas, who will go to jail with him. Every leader needs a Timothy, someone they can pour their life into and send to do the work they are not able to do.

In unity, we recognize that we are who we are because of someone else. We stand on the shoulders of those who have gone before us, and we have a responsibility to lift others as we climb. Unity and teamwork are not just about working together; they are about growing together, supporting each other, and fulfilling the collective purpose God has given us.

Application

Reflect on the principles of unity and teamwork in your own life and within your team or community. Are there areas where you can improve cooperation, submission, or alignment with shared vision and values? Consider how you can foster a spirit of unity that leads to combined determination and greater effectiveness.

Spend time in prayer, asking God to help you and your team grow in unity. Pray for the strength to confront issues with love, the humility to submit to one another, and the wisdom to align with the vision and values that God has given you.

Challenge Questions

1. How can you cultivate a spirit of cooperation within your team or community? What steps can you take to ensure that everyone is working together toward the same goals?

2. In what ways can you encourage a willingness to be confronted and to submit to one another? How can this lead to greater unity and effectiveness within your team?

3. How can you align your team's vision and values to ensure consistency and focus? What practical steps can you take to reinforce these principles regularly?

By understanding and applying these principles of unity and teamwork, we can build stronger, more effective teams that are equipped to fulfill God's purpose in our lives and in our communities. Let's commit to working together in unity, knowing that God's blessing and power are found in our agreement and cooperation.

Day 43:

Qualities of Consistency

Consistency is a cornerstone of success in any area of life. It is not merely about doing something repeatedly but about doing it with purpose, persistence, and discipline. The greatest challenge to maintaining consistency often comes in the form of problems. Problems are inevitable, and they play a crucial role in shaping our character and our path to success. We were not designed to live problem-free lives; instead, we are like tools in the hands of the Master Builder, being used and shaped through our experiences to fulfill our purpose.

Developing consistency in our lives requires certain character qualities that are honed in the midst of life's challenges. Authentic promotion and growth come from maintaining focus and consistency, even when circumstances are less than ideal. Consistency is a form of persistence, and persistence requires discipline. It's time we shift from being motivated only by inspiration and start being moved by the needs and challenges we face.

Here are a few essential qualities of consistency that can help guide us through life's inevitable problems:

1. Anticipate Problems

"The prudent see danger and take refuge, but the simple keep going and pay the penalty." (Proverbs 22:3)

Problems are more accessible to solve if they are anticipated. This doesn't mean we should expect problems to happen with a negative outlook, but rather that we should plan ahead so we are prepared if and when they do arise. A consistent person is proactive rather than reactive. They approach life with the understanding that challenges will come, and they equip themselves to handle these challenges effectively.

A problem solver is someone who has faith and hope for the best but plans for the worst. Anticipation allows us to stay one step ahead, ensuring that we are not caught off guard by the problems that life inevitably brings. By anticipating potential obstacles, we can develop strategies to overcome them before they escalate into more significant issues.

2. Accept the Truth

"Then you will know the truth, and the truth will set you free." (John 8:32)

Many people respond to problems by refusing to accept them. They ignore the issues, hoping they will go away on their own. However, this approach only allows problems to grow and fester. Consistency requires a willingness to face reality, no matter how uncomfortable it may be.

The bills won't get paid if you don't open the envelopes, and life's problems won't be solved if you don't acknowledge them. Accepting the truth means recognizing that you live in a world where problems exist and that these problems must be faced head-on. Denial only delays the inevitable and often makes the situation worse. A person who is consistent in their actions understands the importance of dealing with issues as they arise rather than burying their head in the sand.

3. See the Big Picture

"I press on toward the goal to win the prize for which God has called me heavenward in Christ Jesus." (Philippians 3:14)

A key quality of consistency is the ability to see the big picture. While many people get bogged down by the obstacles in front of them, a person of consistency keeps their eyes on the objectives. The big picture is not about the immediate challenges but about the ultimate goal. Consistent people understand that the journey may be filled with bumps and detours, but the destination is worth the effort.

The objectives are the things that must be completed to achieve the bigger goal. By continually focusing on the end product, we are motivated to push through the small, daily tasks that lead to success. Being faithful to the small things allows us to be trusted with more significant responsibilities. As Luke 16:10 reminds us, "Whoever can be trusted with very little can also be trusted with much, and whoever is dishonest with very little will also be dishonest with much." By keeping the big picture in mind, we ensure that our efforts, no matter how small, are contributing to something greater.

4. Handle One Problem at a Time

"Therefore do not worry about tomorrow, for tomorrow will worry about itself. Each day has enough trouble of its own." (Matthew 6:34)

Consistency in dealing with problems means handling them one at a time. Problems are rarely solved all at once. Instead, they must be tackled step by step, with patience and persistence. A consistent person knows how to prioritize issues and address them in the order of importance.

By breaking down problems into manageable parts, we prevent ourselves from becoming overwhelmed. Lining up problems by priority and attacking them one by one allows us to maintain focus and ensures that each issue receives the attention it deserves. This approach also helps us avoid the paralysis that can come from trying to solve everything at once.

Application

Reflect on your own approach to consistency. Do you find yourself easily derailed by problems, or are you able to maintain focus despite the challenges? Consider how you can apply these qualities of consistency to your daily life. Begin by anticipating potential problems and developing strategies to address them. Commit to accepting the truth of your circumstances, no matter how difficult, and focus on the big picture rather than getting lost in the details. Finally, practice handling one problem at a time, prioritizing it, and dealing with each issue as it arises.

Spend time in prayer, asking God to help you develop these qualities of consistency. Pray for the strength to face challenges head-on, the wisdom to see the big picture, and the patience to handle problems one at a time. Trust that as you grow in consistency, you will become more effective in fulfilling the purpose God has for your life.

Challenge Questions

1. How can you better anticipate potential problems in your life and prepare for them? What steps can you take to be more proactive rather than reactive?

2. Are there areas in your life where you have been avoiding the truth? How can you confront these issues and begin to address them with consistency?

3. What is the big picture in your life? How can you keep your focus on your ultimate goals, even when faced with daily challenges?

4. How can you prioritize problems in your life and address them one at a time? What strategies can you implement to ensure that you handle issues with focus and persistence?

By cultivating these qualities of consistency, you will not only overcome the problems in your life but also grow more robust and more resilient in your journey toward fulfilling your God-given purpose.

Day 44:

The Weakest Link

Our God is a corporate God. He created Adam and noticed that it was not good for him to be alone, so He created Eve, forming the first team. This was the beginning of God's ongoing work through teams. Throughout creation, the concept of teamwork is essential for survival and purpose. From the insect world to the animal kingdom, everything that lives depends on a system of teamwork. Within these systems, one component can make everything go wrong. The strength of a team is always impacted by its weakest link. No matter how one tries to cover it up, a weak link will eventually reveal itself.

The process of assembling and maintaining a team can be challenging. When building a team, there are some crucial factors to consider, and understanding these factors is essential to ensuring that the team remains strong and effective.

1. Not Everyone Will Make the Journey

"But the one who stands firm to the end will be saved." (Matthew 24:13)

Not everyone who starts the journey with you will be able to finish it. This reality is valid in all areas of life, including the Kingdom of God. As you move forward in pursuing God's purpose, you will encounter people who, for various reasons, cannot continue with you. Some will not be able to conquer new territories, and others may resist the growth and change required to fulfill the vision.

It's essential to recognize that this is not necessarily a reflection of a person's value or worth but rather an acknowledgment that different people have different roles to play. Some are meant to start the journey with you but may not be equipped to see it through to the end. Understanding this can help you make difficult decisions when it comes to ensuring that your team remains strong and focused on the mission.

2. Not Everyone Should Take the Journey

"Enter through the narrow gate. For wide is the gate and broad is the road that leads to destruction, and many enter through it." (Matthew 7:13)

The journey of fulfilling God's purpose is a calling, not something everyone will choose to undertake. It's not the popular thing to do, and it's not for everyone. Some people are not called to take the journey with you, and trying to bring them along can weaken the team. The narrow path is often lonely, requiring perseverance, faith, and a deep commitment to God's calling.

When assembling a team, it's crucial to discern who is genuinely called to join you on the journey. Those who are called will be willing to make the sacrifices necessary to achieve the vision, while those who are not called may struggle to keep up, potentially becoming a weak link in the team.

3. Not Everyone Can Take the Journey

"No one who puts a hand to the plow and looks back is fit for service in the kingdom of God." (Luke 9:62)

Some people may want to take the journey with you, but they simply cannot keep the pace. They may lack the capacity to grow with the team, adjust to new challenges, or see the big picture. These individuals may have good intentions, but their inability to keep up can hinder the progress of the entire team.

It's essential to evaluate the strengths and weaknesses of each team member honestly. If someone cannot meet the demands of the journey, it may be necessary to make difficult decisions for the greater good of the mission. This is not about rejecting people but about ensuring that the team remains strong and capable of fulfilling its purpose.

4. Teams are Vital to the Growth of the Kingdom of God

"As iron sharpens iron, so one person sharpens another." (Proverbs 27:17)

No one man or woman can fulfill his or her purpose in isolation. We were created for community, and the development of a team is crucial to advancing the Kingdom of God. Each member of the team plays a vital role in sharpening and supporting one another. However, for the team to be effective, it must be strong and unified, with no weak links.

When developing a team, it's essential to foster a culture of mutual accountability and growth. Each member must be committed to personal and collective growth, and there must be a willingness to address weaknesses openly and constructively. This kind of environment ensures that the team remains strong and capable of achieving its mission.

Application

Take a moment to evaluate the teams you are a part of, whether in your church, workplace, or personal life. Consider whether there are any weak links that need to be addressed and how you can contribute to strengthening the team. Reflect on your own role within the team—are you fully committed to the journey, or are there areas where you need to grow?

Spend time in prayer, asking God for wisdom in assembling and leading teams. Pray for discernment to recognize who is called to join you on the journey and who may need to step aside. Ask for the strength to make difficult decisions that will ultimately benefit the mission and for the grace to support and encourage one another as you work together to fulfill God's purpose.

Challenge Questions

1. Who are the key members of the teams you are a part of? Are they fully committed to the journey, or are there areas where they may be struggling?

2. How can you constructively address any weak links within your team? What steps can you take to ensure that the team remains strong and focused on the mission?

3. Are you fulfilling your role within the team to the best of your ability? What areas of growth or development do you need to focus on to contribute more effectively to the team?

4. What steps can you take to foster a culture of mutual accountability and growth within your team? How can you encourage open and constructive communication among team members?

By understanding and addressing the dynamics of teamwork, you can ensure that your team remains strong, unified, and capable of fulfilling its purpose in the Kingdom of God. Remember, the strength of a team is as strong as its weakest link, and by working together, you can overcome any challenges and achieve great things for God's glory.

Day 45:

The Trap of Motivation

Motivation is often seen as the key to getting things done. It is an internal condition that activates behavior and gives it direction, energizing and directing goal-oriented actions. Some people seem to thrive on motivation, needing it to start any task, while others push forward with little of it, relying more on discipline and routine. In understanding motivation, one critical insight emerges: motivation alone is never enough to get you started—don't wait for it! It was not designed to start you but to keep you going once you have begun.

Types of Motivation

When it comes to motivation, there are generally two types of people:

1.   Those who feel good BEFORE they do something:

• These individuals often need to feel inspired or motivated before they begin a task. They might wait for the perfect moment, a burst of inspiration, or some external encouragement before they start working toward their goals.

• This approach can be limiting because motivation is often fleeting and inconsistent. Relying solely on feeling good before taking action can lead to procrastination and missed opportunities.

2.   Those who do something BEFORE they feel good:

• These people understand that action precedes motivation. They start working on their tasks even when they don't feel particularly inspired or motivated.

• By doing so, they often find that motivation follows action. The act of starting creates momentum, and that momentum fuels further motivation.

The Illusion of Motivation

Many people fall into the trap of waiting for motivation to strike before they act. They believe that they need to feel motivated to begin working on their goals, whether it's losing weight, pursuing a career, or making positive changes in their lives. However, this mindset can be a significant barrier to progress.

The truth is that motivation is not a magical force that will suddenly appear and propel you into action. It's more like a by-product that comes after you've already started doing the right thing. The idea that you need to feel motivated before you can begin is a trap that can keep you stuck in inaction.

Taking Action Without Motivation

An excerpt from a medical magazine highlights this concept effectively:

"Motivation is not going to strike you like lightning. Motivation is not something that someone else—a nurse, doctor, or family member—can bestow or force on you. The whole idea of motivation is a trap.

Forget motivation. Just do it. Exercise, lose weight, test your blood sugar, or whatever. Do it without motivation. And then, guess what? After you start doing the right thing, that's when motivation comes in, and it makes it easy for you to keep on doing it.

Motivation is like love and happiness. It's a by-product. When you're actively engaged in DOING SOMETHING, it sneaks up and zaps you when you least expect it."

This passage emphasizes the importance of taking action, regardless of whether you feel motivated at the moment. By starting to do what you know you should, motivation will often follow as a natural consequence of your actions. This aligns with the insight from Harvard psychologist Jerome Bruner, who says, **"You're more likely to act yourself into feeling than feel yourself into action."**

Biblical Insights on Action and Motivation

The Bible also supports the idea that action precedes feeling or motivation. James 1:22 (NIV) says, "Do not merely listen to the word, and so deceive yourselves. Do what it says." This verse encourages believers to act on their faith, not just listen passively. The act of doing, in this context, is what leads to growth and spiritual fulfillment.

In another passage, Philippians 2:13 (NIV) states, "For it is God who works in you to will and to act in order to fulfill his good purpose." Here, Paul emphasizes that God empowers us to act according to His will. God gives us the willingness to act, but the action itself is still our responsibility. This shows that divine guidance often requires our active participation, even when we don't feel like it.

Application

The next time you find yourself waiting for motivation to strike before you start something meaningful, remind yourself that action comes first. Don't let the trap of motivation keep you from making progress. Begin the task at hand, whether it's a spiritual discipline, a personal goal, or a work-related project, and trust that motivation will follow your initial efforts.

Start your day with action. Even if you don't feel like it, begin with small steps, such as reading a passage of Scripture, praying, or working on a task you've been putting off. As you do, you'll likely find that the act of starting creates a sense of motivation that wasn't there before.

Challenge Questions

1. In what areas of your life have you been waiting for motivation to start? How can you take the first step today, regardless of how you feel?

2. How can you apply the principle of action preceding motivation in your spiritual life? What spiritual disciplines can you start practicing even when you don't feel particularly motivated?

3. Reflect on a time when you took action despite lacking motivation. What were the results, and how did it impact your perspective on taking initiative in other areas of your life?

4. How can you encourage others in your community or family to overcome the trap of motivation? What advice or support can you offer to help them take the first step?

By understanding that motivation is not a prerequisite for action but often a result of it, you can break free from the trap of waiting for the perfect moment to begin. Take the initiative, trust that motivation will follow, and experience the growth and progress that come from consistent, purposeful action.

Day 46:

Goals and Success

Yesterday, during our leadership meeting, we engaged in a team-building exercise that involved setting and achieving goals. The game required our team to unite, collaborate, and motivate each other to reach the benchmarks that I had set for them. As they accomplished one goal, I introduced even steeper ones, challenging them to push further. The exercise was not just about the game; it was a practical lesson in the importance of goal-setting and teamwork. It also prepared them for the actual goals I have set for them to achieve by December.

The Power of Goals

One of the most powerful actions we can take to change our future is setting clear goals and working diligently to achieve them every day. The truth is that a person of average intelligence who has clear goals will outperform a genius who isn't sure what they really want. Goals provide direction and focus, turning dreams into reality.

Setting goals is more than just writing down what you want to achieve; it's about creating a roadmap for success. Without goals, you can easily drift through life without any sense of direction or purpose. However, when you have specific, measurable, achievable, relevant, and time-bound (SMART) goals, you set yourself up for success.

Proverbs 16:3 (NIV) says, "Commit to the Lord whatever you do, and he will establish your plans." This verse emphasizes the importance of aligning your goals with God's will. When you commit your plans to the Lord, He guides your steps and helps you achieve success in your endeavors.

The Ingredients of Success

Success is the achievement of intention, the accomplishment of goals, and the victory in whatever you set out to do. However, success requires two essential elements:

1. You must know precisely what you want.

Clarity is crucial. Without a clear vision of what you want to achieve, you'll struggle to make progress. Successful people have a vivid picture of their goals and a strong desire to reach them.

2. You must be willing to pay the price to achieve what you want.

Success doesn't come without sacrifice. Whether it's time, effort, resources, or comfort, achieving your goals often requires paying a price. This could mean working late hours, giving up leisure time, or investing in education or training.

Luke 14:28 (NIV) underscores the importance of planning and commitment: "Suppose one of you wants to build a tower. Won't you first sit down and estimate the cost to see if you have enough money to complete it?" This scripture reminds us that success requires careful planning and a willingness to invest in what's necessary to achieve our goals.

The Law of Focus

We become what we think about most of the time. This simple yet profound truth highlights the importance of focus in achieving success. The law of focus is not complicated to attain; in fact, we live it every day as we direct our thoughts and attention toward various aspects of our lives. However, the challenge arises when we have to pay a price to achieve what we truly desire.

Philippians 4:8 (NIV) provides guidance on where our focus should be: "Finally, brothers and sisters, whatever is true, whatever is noble, whatever is right, whatever is pure, whatever is lovely, whatever is admirable—if anything is excellent or praiseworthy—think about such things." Focusing on positive, goal-oriented thoughts helps us stay on track and move closer to success.

Successful people are those who continually think about what they want and how to get it. They set goals and work toward them with determination and perseverance. On the other hand, unsuccessful people tend to focus on what they don't like or want, letting their fears, concerns, and worries dominate their thoughts. This negative focus prevents them from moving forward and achieving their goals.

Application

Take some time to reflect on your goals for this week, month, or year. If you don't have any goals set, now is the time to create them. Start by identifying what you truly want to achieve, and then break those goals down into actionable steps. Remember, it's not just about setting goals but also about being willing to pay the price to achieve them.

Commit your goals to the Lord, asking for His guidance and strength as you work toward them. Keep your focus on what you want to achieve rather than on your fears or obstacles. With clarity, commitment, and God's help, you can reach your goals and find success.

Challenge Questions

1. What specific goals have you set for yourself in the next week, month, or year? If you haven't set any, take some time today to write them down.

2. Are your goals aligned with God's will for your life? How can you commit your plans to the Lord and seek His guidance in achieving them?

3. What sacrifices are you willing to make to achieve your goals? Are there areas where you need to increase your focus or effort to reach your desired outcome?

4. How can you shift your focus from your fears and concerns to your goals and the actions needed to achieve them? What practical steps can you take today to move closer to your goals?

By setting clear goals, focusing on them, and being willing to pay the price to achieve them, you position yourself for success. Remember, with God's help, all things are possible, and you can accomplish the purpose He has set before you.

Day 47:

Sacrifice?

"Through Jesus, therefore, let us continually offer to God a sacrifice of praise…" (Hebrews 13:15)

In the book of Hebrews, the writer delves deeply into the differences between Judaism and Christianity, emphasizing how the new covenant through Jesus is the fulfillment and perfection of the old. For the Jewish believers, sacrifices were central to their worship and religious identity. The concept of sacrifice—offering something valuable to God—was foundational to their faith. However, the writer of Hebrews challenges these believers to embrace a new perspective on sacrifice: one that is rooted in the continuous offering of praise through Jesus Christ.

The Essence of Sacrifice

In its essence, sacrifice involves giving up something of value and surrendering it to a higher purpose or authority. True worship, in the biblical sense, is intrinsically linked to sacrifice. Throughout the Old Testament, the act of worship was almost always accompanied by the offering of sacrifices, which represented the worshiper's devotion, repentance, and reverence toward God.

But what qualifies as a true sacrifice in the context of our Christian faith? Is it merely the act of giving up our time, resources, or comfort? The writer of Hebrews suggests that through Jesus, our understanding of sacrifice is transformed. We are called to continually offer a "sacrifice of praise," indicating that our praise itself—especially when it costs us something—is a powerful form of worship.

Challenging Our Perception of Sacrifice

Reflecting on the idea of sacrifice, it's important to ask ourselves: What are we truly sacrificing for God? Is it simply our spare time, leftover resources, or minimal effort? Sometimes, we may fall into the trap of thinking that giving up small conveniences or making minor adjustments is a great sacrifice. But is that really the kind of sacrifice God desires?

Consider this: if we always receive more than we give up, have we truly sacrificed anything? This question challenges us to re-evaluate what it means to sacrifice in our walk with God. The reality is that God has given us everything—our time, talents, and resources. When we give back to Him, we are not losing anything but instead investing in His kingdom, which yields far greater returns than anything we could imagine.

The Call to True Sacrifice

True sacrifice involves more than just giving from our surplus. It requires us to offer something that genuinely costs us, something that reflects our devotion and surrender to God. The essence of sacrifice is not found in the quantity or size of the offering but in the heart and intention behind it.

Romans 12:1 (NIV) says, "Therefore, I urge you, brothers and sisters, in view of God's mercy, to offer your bodies as a living sacrifice, holy and pleasing to God—this is your true and proper worship." This verse captures the idea that our entire lives should be a continuous act of worship and sacrifice. It's not just about the moments we spend in prayer, worship, or church activities but about living every aspect of our lives as an offering to God.

Application

As we reflect on the concept of sacrifice, let's challenge ourselves to go beyond the superficial. Here are some ways to apply this teaching in our daily lives:

Evaluate Your Offerings: Take a moment to assess what you are offering to God. Are you giving Him your best, or just what is convenient? Consider how you can offer a "sacrifice of praise" that genuinely reflects your devotion.

Sacrifice in Worship: Worship involves more than just singing songs. It's about offering our hearts, minds, and bodies to God. Think about how you can deepen your worship by incorporating acts of service, generosity, and obedience into your daily routine.

Kill the Distractions: Identify the things in your life that distract you from fully committing to God. Whether it's laziness, procrastination, or misplaced priorities, ask God to help you "kill" these distractions so that you can offer Him true worship.

Live Sacrificially: Consider how you can live sacrificially in your relationships, work, and personal life. This might mean giving more of your time, resources, or energy to serve others and advance God's kingdom.

Challenge Questions

1. What does true sacrifice look like in your life? How can you move beyond giving out of convenience and offer something that truly costs you?

2. In what areas of your life have you been giving God your leftovers instead of your best? How can you prioritize your time, resources, and energy to honor God more fully?

3. How can you incorporate the idea of "sacrifice of praise" into your daily routine? What practical steps can you take to ensure that your worship is not just a ritual but a genuine offering to God?

4. Are there distractions or attitudes that prevent you from fully surrendering to God? What can you do to overcome these obstacles and offer your life as a living sacrifice?

As we reflect on the true meaning of sacrifice, let's commit to offering God our best—our time, energy, resources, and hearts. When we do, we will experience the fullness of His presence and the power of living a life fully surrendered to Him.

Day 48:

The Application Problem

In today's world, we're surrounded by a vast array of information. The age of the internet has made knowledge more accessible than ever before. We have resources at our fingertips to educate ourselves on virtually any subject, from financial literacy to spiritual growth. Yet, despite this abundance of information, we still struggle with a fundamental issue that no amount of technology can solve: the problem of application.

The Gap Between Knowledge and Action

It's often said that "knowledge is power." However, knowledge in itself is not powerful until it is applied. This is where many of us fall short. We read, listen, and learn, but when it comes to putting what we've learned into practice, we hesitate, procrastinate, or simply ignore the call to action. The result? We become well-informed but unchanged. We know what we should do, but the doing part—applying that knowledge—is where the breakdown occurs.

In the book of James, this principle is clearly illustrated:

"Do not merely listen to the word, and so deceive yourselves. Do what it says." (James 1:22)

This scripture reminds us that hearing the word, or even agreeing with it, is not enough. True transformation comes from application. Without it, our faith is stagnant, and our knowledge remains theoretical rather than practical.

The Importance of Application

Application is the bridge between knowledge and transformation. It's one thing to nod in agreement during a sermon or to take copious notes during a seminar, but it's another to live out those teachings in our daily lives. The real challenge lies in making the principles we learn a part of our everyday actions and decisions.

Consider the parable of the wise and foolish builders:

"Therefore everyone who hears these words of mine and puts them into practice is like a wise man who built his house on the rock. The rain came down, the streams rose, and the winds blew and beat against that house; yet it did not fall, because it had its foundation on the rock. But everyone who hears these words of mine and does not put them into practice is like a foolish man who built his house on sand." (Matthew 7:24-26)

Jesus emphasized the importance of not just hearing His words but putting them into practice. The stability of our lives, like the house in the parable, depends on our willingness to apply what we learn.

Application as a Discipline

Application is not just about doing what we've learned once or twice; it's about developing a habit, a discipline of consistently living out what we know. This requires intentionality and commitment. Like a soldier who signs up for the military, applying knowledge means committing to a path of practice, training, and often sacrifice.

The Apostle Paul understood this concept well. He likened the Christian life to running a race:

"Do you not know that in a race, all the runners run, but only one gets the prize? Run in such a way as to get the prize. Everyone who competes in the games goes into strict training. They do it to get a crown that will not last, but we do it to get a crown that will last forever." (1 Corinthians 9:24-25)

Paul's analogy shows that success in the Christian life, just like in athletics, comes from strict training and discipline. This training is the consistent application of God's word in our lives.

Overcoming the Application Problem

So, how do we overcome the application problem? How do we move from being hearers of the word to doers of the word? Here are a few practical steps:

1. **Start Small, but Start Now:** The application doesn't have to be overwhelming. Begin with small, manageable actions. Whether it's setting aside time each day to pray, applying a biblical principle to

a problematic situation, or starting a new habit, the key is to begin. Small steps lead to significant changes over time.

2. Set Clear Goals: Just as in any other area of life, setting clear, achievable goals helps us to apply what we've learned. For example, if your goal is to be more generous, start by setting a specific amount you will give each month, and track your progress.

3. Accountability: Share your goals with someone you trust. Accountability partners can help keep you on track, provide encouragement, and gently remind you when you start to slip.

4. Reflect and Adjust: Regularly take time to reflect on your progress. Are you applying what you've learned? What obstacles are you facing? What adjustments can you make to improve?

Prayer: Ask God for the strength and wisdom to apply His word in your life. The Holy Spirit is our helper, guiding us and empowering us to live out the truths we know.

Application

As we reflect on the challenge of applying what we learn, let's commit to being doers of the word, not just hearers. Here's how you can begin to bridge the gap between knowledge and action:

Evaluate: Take an honest look at your life. Are there areas where you've accumulated knowledge but haven't yet applied it? Identify these areas and make a plan to start using what you know.

Commit: Make a commitment to consistent application. Whether it's a spiritual discipline like prayer or a practical step like budgeting, commit to applying what you've learned regularly.

Ask for Help: Don't try to do it all alone. Seek the support of your community, whether it's a small group, a mentor, or an accountability partner.

Challenge Questions

1. What areas of your life have you been learning but not applying? What steps can you take this week to begin applying that knowledge?

2. How can you develop a habit of consistent application in your spiritual life? What practical changes can you make to ensure you're not just hearing the word but living it out?

3. Who can you ask to hold you accountable in your application journey? How can you support someone else in their application journey?

4. What small step can you take today to start bridging the gap between what you know and what you do? Reflect on one area where you've been hesitant to apply what you've learned and commit to taking action.

Let's move beyond simply gathering information and step into the transformative power of application, knowing that the sacrifices we make today will yield great rewards in the future.

Day 49:

Momentary Afflictions

We often face mountains, obstacles, and storms in our lives that seem overwhelming and insurmountable. However, the Bible teaches us that God's provision and purpose are often found on the other side of these challenges. Just as Abraham climbed one side of the mountain while his provision was on the other, we, too, must trust that God is working on our behalf, even when we cannot see it.

Consider the disciples' experience in Mark 6:45-56. They were crossing the lake, struggling against the wind and waves, and rowing for their lives. It was only after Jesus showed up that they learned a profound lesson on faith. What they didn't know was that on the other side of that storm lay Gennesaret, the place where Jesus would perform some of His greatest miracles. This story illustrates that our journey in life will inevitably come with momentary afflictions. Yet, on the other side of these afflictions, we find our purpose, provision, direction, and power.

The Purpose of Momentary Afflictions

These momentary afflictions serve a greater purpose in our lives. They are not just random challenges but are designed by God to reveal various aspects of our spiritual walk. It is through these trials that we can better gauge our spiritual growth and understanding of the kingdom of God.

In 2 Corinthians 4:17, Paul reminds us, **"For our light and momentary troubles are achieving for us an eternal glory that far outweighs them all."** This verse is a powerful reminder that the difficulties we face are temporary and are working towards a far greater purpose.

What Momentary Afflictions Reveal About Us

1. **The Level of Our Faith**

Momentary afflictions test and reveal the proper level of our faith. It is easy to have faith when everything is going well, but the real test comes when we face challenges. Do we still trust God when the storms of life are raging? These trials help us see where our faith truly stands.

Scripture: *"Consider it pure joy, my brothers and sisters, whenever you face trials of many kinds because you know that the testing of your faith produces perseverance."* (James 1:2-3)

2. The Strength of Our Commitment

Our commitment to God and His purposes is also tested during times of affliction. Are we committed to following Him, even when it's difficult? These moments reveal whether our commitment is superficial or deeply rooted in our love for God.

Scripture: *"But the one who stands firm to the end will be saved."* (Matthew 24:13)

3. The Level of Our Maturity

Spiritual maturity is not measured by how much we know but by how we respond to life's challenges. Mature believers are those who can endure hardship with grace and patience, trusting in God's plan even when it's not clear. Afflictions reveal the depth of our maturity in Christ.

Scripture: *"Not only so, but we also glory in our sufferings, because we know that suffering produces perseverance; perseverance, character; and character, hope."* (Romans 5:3-4)

4. The Health of Our Attitude

Our attitude during difficult times is a strong indicator of our spiritual health. Do we complain and grumble, or do we maintain a positive outlook, trusting that God is in control? A healthy attitude reflects a heart that is aligned with God's will, even in the midst of trials.

Scripture: *"Do everything without grumbling or arguing, so that you may become blameless and pure, 'children of God without fault in a warped and crooked generation.'"* (Philippians 2:14-15)

5. Our Ability to Be Taught

Finally, momentary afflictions reveal our teachability. Are we willing to learn from our trials, allowing them to shape us into the people God wants us to be? Or do we resist and refuse to grow? Being teachable is essential for spiritual growth and maturity.

Scripture: *"My son, do not despise the Lord's discipline, and do not resent his rebuke, because the Lord disciplines those he loves, as a father the son he delights in."* (Proverbs 3:11-12)

Application

Understanding the purpose of momentary afflictions can help us navigate life's challenges with a renewed perspective. Here's how you can apply these insights to your life:

Reflect on Your Faith: When you face challenges, take a moment to reflect on your faith. Are you trusting God in the midst of your trials? How can you strengthen your faith during these times?

Examine Your Commitment: Consider your level of commitment to God. Are you fully committed to following Him, even when it's difficult? What steps can you take to deepen your commitment?

Assess Your Maturity: Use your trials as an opportunity to assess your spiritual maturity. How do you respond to challenges? Are you growing in character and perseverance?

Check Your Attitude: Pay attention to your attitude during difficult times. Are you maintaining a positive outlook, or do you find yourself grumbling and complaining? How can you cultivate a healthier mindset?

Embrace Teachability: Be open to learning from your afflictions. Ask God to show you what He wants to teach you through your trials, and be willing to grow and change.

Challenge Questions

1. **How do you typically respond to momentary afflictions?** What do your responses reveal about your faith, commitment, maturity, attitude, and teachability?

2. **In what areas of your life do you need to strengthen your faith in the midst of trials?** How can you actively work on deepening your trust in God during challenging times?

3. **What practical steps can you take to maintain a positive attitude during challenges?** How can you shift your focus from the temporary afflictions to the eternal glory that awaits?

4. **Are you open to learning from your afflictions, or do you resist change?** How can you develop a more teachable spirit that allows God to work in and through your trials?

By understanding and embracing the purpose of momentary afflictions, we can navigate life's challenges with grace, knowing that they are preparing us for a greater glory that far outweighs them all. Let's fix our eyes on what is unseen, trusting that God is using every trial to shape us into the people He has called us to be.

Day 50:

The Passion of Philippians

The Epistle to the Philippians stands out as one of the most passionate and ardent letters in the New Testament. Written from a prison cell, the Apostle Paul, inspired by the Holy Spirit, infused this letter with charges and challenges designed to elevate our passion and pursuit of Christ, especially during difficult times. The fervor and obsession for the cause of the Gospel resonate throughout its verses, making it a powerful source of encouragement for believers who are serious about their faith. This letter is not for the faint of heart; it's for those who are ready to embrace the challenges of living a Christ-centered life. Here are 12 challenges I've received from Philippians; follow these, and you'll never experience defeat!

1. Never Lose Confidence in the Work That the Lord Began in You

"Being confident of this, that he who began a good work in you will carry it on to completion until the day of Christ Jesus." (Philippians 1:6)

Paul reminds us that the work God started in us is not just a temporary project but a lifelong process that He is committed to completing. No matter how difficult the journey may seem, we can be confident that God is continually working in us, shaping us to fulfill His purposes.

2. Always Expect Every Situation to Turn Out for the Good!

"Yes, and I will continue to rejoice, for I know that through your prayers and the help given by the Spirit of Jesus Christ, what has happened to me will turn out for my deliverance." (Philippians 1:19)

Even in dire circumstances, Paul maintained an expectation that God would bring about good. This mindset is essential for believers. When we trust in God's sovereignty, we can rejoice, knowing that He is working all things together for our good and His glory.

3. Never Allow Satan to Intimidate You

"Without being frightened in any way by those who oppose you. This is a sign to them that they will be destroyed, but that you will be saved—and that by God." (Philippians 1:28)

Paul encourages us to stand firm in our faith, refusing to be intimidated by opposition. Our courage in the face of adversity is a testimony to others of the power of God at work in our lives.

4. Always Stay Humble Before the Lord and Expect Him to Exalt You in Due Season

"Your attitude should be the same as that of Christ Jesus: Who, being in very nature God, did not consider equality with God something to be grasped, but made himself nothing, taking the very nature of a servant…" (Philippians 2:5-7)

Humility is a hallmark of the Christian life. By following Christ's example of humility, we position ourselves for God's exaltation in His perfect timing.

5. Never Let Go of God's Word, No Matter How Impossible Your Situation May Look

"As you hold out the word of life—in order that I may boast on the day of Christ that I did not run or labor for nothing." (Philippians 2:16)

Holding fast to God's Word is crucial, especially when circumstances seem impossible. God's promises are our anchor in the storm, and by clinging to them, we demonstrate our faith and trust in His plans.

6. Always Protect Yourself from Deception

"Watch out for those dogs, those men who do evil, those mutilators of the flesh." (Philippians 3:2)

Paul warns us to be vigilant against deception. In a world full of false teachings and distractions, we must remain grounded in the truth of God's Word to avoid being led astray.

7. Never Hang On to Your Past. Keep Reaching Forward

"Not that I have already obtained all this, or have already been made perfect, but I press on to take hold of that for which Christ Jesus took hold of me." (Philippians 3:12)

The Christian life is a journey of continual growth. Paul encourages us to forget what is behind us and press on toward the goal of becoming more like Christ, embracing the future He has for us.

8. Always Maintain Your Joy

"Rejoice in the Lord always. I will say it again: Rejoice!" (Philippians 4:4)

Joy is a choice, and Paul urges us to choose joy in every circumstance. By rejoicing in the Lord, we demonstrate our trust in His goodness and faithfulness.

9. Pray and Pray Again and Manage Your Thought Life

"Do not be anxious about anything, but in everything, by prayer and petition, with thanksgiving, present your requests to God. And the peace of God, which transcends all understanding, will guard your hearts and your minds in Christ Jesus." (Philippians 4:6-7)

Prayer is the key to managing anxiety and maintaining peace. Paul instructs us to bring everything to God in prayer, trusting that His peace will guard our hearts and minds.

10. Never Quit!

"I can do all things through Christ who gives me strength." (Philippians 4:13)

Perseverance is essential in the Christian walk. Paul reminds us that we can do all things through Christ's strength, encouraging us to keep going, even when the road is tough.

11. Never Stop Giving. Keep Planting Seeds of Faith

"And my God will meet all your needs according to his glorious riches in Christ Jesus." (Philippians 4:19)

Generosity is a reflection of our trust in God's provision. Paul assures us that God will supply all our needs as we continue to give and plant seeds of faith.

12. Always Look to God as Your Source of Supply

"And my God will meet all your needs according to his glorious riches in Christ Jesus." (Philippians 4:19)

God is our ultimate provider. Paul encourages us to look to Him as the source of all our needs, trusting that He will provide in His perfect timing.

Application

The book of Philippians is not just a letter; it's a blueprint for victorious Christian living. By embracing the challenges laid out in this epistle, we can develop a faith that is resilient, joyful, and steadfast. Each of these principles invites us to go deeper in our walk with Christ, relying on His strength and wisdom to navigate life's challenges.

Challenge Questions:

1. Which of the 12 challenges in Philippians resonates most with your current season of life? Why?

2. How can you apply the principle of maintaining joy in difficult circumstances this week?

3. In what ways can you protect yourself from deception and stay grounded in the truth of God's Word?

4. Reflect on a time when you saw God's provision after remaining faithful through a difficult situation. How did this experience strengthen your faith?

By living out the principles in Philippians, we not only align ourselves with God's will but also position ourselves to experience the fullness of life that He has promised. Let's strive to live out these challenges with passion and perseverance, knowing that through Christ, we will never experience defeat.

Day 51:

Commitment

"Continue to work out your salvation with fear and trembling, for it is God who works in you to will and to do of his good purpose." (Philippians 2:12-13)

Commitment to the cause of Christ is not just a casual decision; it is a life-altering dedication that molds us into the likeness of Christ. The process of becoming more like Christ is intrinsically tied to our willingness to commit to His cause, His commands, and His calling. When we commit ourselves to Him, we enter into a partnership where we work out our salvation, and God works within us to fulfill His purpose.

The Power of Commitment

Commitment has a transformative power that goes beyond simple determination or willpower. It is the foundation of spiritual maturity, integrity, and character. As believers, our spiritual growth and development are directly linked to the commitments we make in our walk with God. It is through these commitments that we begin to experience the depth and richness of our relationship with Christ.

1. Commitment Dares Us to Get Rid of Old Routines

"Do not conform to the pattern of this world, but be transformed by the renewing of your mind. Then you will be able to test and approve what God's will is—his good, pleasing, and perfect will." (Romans 12:2)

One of the first things that commitment does is challenge us to break away from old, unproductive routines. These routines may have been part of our lives for years, but they no longer serve us in our walk with Christ. Commitment pushes us to evaluate our habits and make the necessary changes to align our lives with God's will. It's a daring act of faith to step out of the comfort zone of the familiar and embrace the unknown, trusting that God's plans are better than our old ways.

2. Commitment Develops New Habits

"Therefore, if anyone is in Christ, the new creation has come: The old has gone, the new is here!" (2 Corinthians 5:17)

As we commit to the cause of Christ, we begin to form new habits that reflect our new identity in Him. These habits are not just about behavior modification; they are about creating a new belief system rooted in the truth of God's Word. Commitment helps us to establish practices that cultivate spiritual growth, such as daily prayer, studying Scripture, and engaging in community with other believers. Over time, these new habits become ingrained in our lives, leading us to a deeper and more meaningful relationship with God.

3. Commitment as a Covenant of Exchange

"But seek first his kingdom and his righteousness, and all these things will be given to you as well." (Matthew 6:33)

Understanding commitment also involves recognizing it as a covenant of exchange. In a marriage, both partners have responsibilities, and the relationship flourishes when each fulfills their part. Similarly, in our commitment to God, we work out our part—obedience, faithfulness, and pursuit of His will—while God works in us to accomplish His purpose. It is a partnership where our efforts meet God's grace, resulting in a life that brings glory to Him. As we work out our salvation with reverence and dedication, God works in us to shape our desires and actions according to His will.

The Role of Commitment in Spiritual Growth

Working out our salvation is not about earning our place in heaven; it is about living out the transformation that God has begun in us. Commitment plays a crucial role in this process because it keeps us focused on the goal of becoming more like Christ. Without commitment, our spiritual growth would be sporadic and shallow. But with commitment, we are constantly moving forward, deepening our faith, and expanding our capacity to reflect Christ in all that we do.

Application

Commitment is more than just a decision; it is a lifestyle. It requires us to be intentional about our choices, disciplined in our habits, and faithful in our walk with God. As you reflect on your own commitments, consider how they are shaping your spiritual journey. Are there old routines that you need to break away from? Are you developing new habits that align with your identity in Christ? Are you fulfilling your part of the covenant with God, trusting Him to work in and through you?

Challenge Questions:

1.   What old routines or habits do you need to break in order to fully commit to God's purpose for your life?

2.   What new habits can you develop to strengthen your commitment to Christ?

3.   How does viewing commitment as a covenant of exchange with God change your perspective on working out your salvation?

4.   In what ways can you actively partner with God to fulfill His purpose for your life?

Commitment to Christ is the pathway to spiritual maturity and fulfillment. As we commit to His cause, we allow Him to work in us, transforming us into the image of His Son and enabling us to live out our salvation with purpose and passion. Let's embrace the power of commitment and experience the fullness of life that God has in store for us.

Day 52:

Architect, Artist, Poet, & Designer

"For we are God's workmanship, created in Christ Jesus to do good works, which God prepared in advance for us to do." (Ephesians 2:10)

Each of us is intricately designed and uniquely formed to fulfill specific tasks and purposes in our lives. Just as an architect meticulously plans a building with its purpose in mind, God, the ultimate Architect, designed each of us with a particular role and function in His grand design. Our lives are not a result of random events but are carefully crafted and purposed by a Creator who knows the end from the beginning.

The Purpose of Design

Before an architect draws the first line or makes the first sketch, they already know what the building's purpose will be. The intended function of a building determines its design and structure. Similarly, before God created each of us, He already decided the role we would play on this earth. Our design is not an accident; it is a reflection of God's intentional purpose for our lives.

"For you created my inmost being; you knit me together in my mother's womb. I praise you because I am fearfully and wonderfully made; your works are wonderful, I know that full well." (Psalm 139:13-14)

The Psalmist David beautifully expresses this truth, acknowledging that every part of our being is fearfully and wonderfully made by God. Our lives, therefore, are not just a series of random events but are part of a divine plan that God carefully orchestrated even before we were born.

God as the Master Designer

God is not only our Architect but also our Artist, Poet, and Designer. He is the Master Designer who has handcrafted each of us as a unique masterpiece. The Greek word used in Ephesians 2:10 for "workmanship" is *poiēma*, from which we derive the English word "poem." This suggests that our lives are like poems, carefully crafted and woven together by God to express His passion, creativity, and purpose.

"Your eyes saw my unformed body. All the days ordained for me were written in your book before one of them came to be." (Psalm 139:16)

Not only did God shape us, but He also planned our lives in advance. Every day we live was written in His book before we even took our first breath. This means that nothing happens in our lives without God's permission. He uses everything we experience—both the good and the bad—to mold and shape us for His service.

The Role of the Architect, Artist, Poet, and Designer

1.   **Architect:** As the Architect of our lives, God has a blueprint for each of us. He knows the exact purpose for which we were created, and He designed us in a way that perfectly suits that purpose. Just as an architect considers the function of a building in its design, God has considered our purpose in every detail of our creation.

2.   **Artist:** God is also the Artist who has painted the canvas of our lives with the colors of His grace, mercy, and love. Each stroke of His brush adds depth, texture, and meaning to our existence. Our lives are His masterpiece, a work of art that reflects His glory.

3.   **Poet:** As the Poet, God has written the story of our lives with poetic precision. Each of us is a verse in the grand poem of creation, a unique expression of His creativity and love. Our lives are meant to be lived out as a beautiful poem, telling the world about the goodness and greatness of our Creator.

4.   **Designer:** Lastly, God is the Designer who has fashioned us with purpose and intention. He has designed our lives in such a way that we can fulfill the good works He prepared in advance for us to do. We are not here by accident; we are here by divine design.

Living Out the Design

Understanding that we are God's workmanship, created for a purpose, should profoundly impact how we live our lives. It means that we are called to walk in the good works that God has prepared for us. It means recognizing that every talent, gift, and ability we have is not for our own benefit but for the fulfillment of God's plan.

"For I know the plans I have for you," declares the Lord, "plans to prosper you and not to harm you, plans to give you hope and a future." (Jeremiah 29:11)

God's plans for us are always for our good and His glory. As we walk in His design, we can trust that He will guide us, provide for us, and fulfill His purposes in our lives.

Application

Reflect on the fact that you are a masterpiece created by God with a specific purpose. Consider how this truth should influence your daily life and decisions. Are you living in a way that aligns with God's design for you? Are you using your gifts and talents to fulfill the good works He has prepared for you?

Challenge Questions:

1.   How does understanding that God is the Architect, Artist, Poet, and Designer of your life change your perspective on your purpose?

2.   In what ways can you actively seek to fulfill the good works that God has prepared for you?

3.   What steps can you take to ensure that you are living according to God's design for your life?

4.   How can you use your unique gifts and talents to reflect God's glory in your daily life?

Remember, you are God's workmanship, created in Christ Jesus for good works. Embrace your design, walk in your purpose, and live out the masterpiece that God has crafted in you.

Conclusion

Reflections on the Journey

As we conclude this 52-day journey of discipleship, it is a fitting moment to pause and consider the path we have traveled together. Each day has offered us insights and challenges, calling us to deepen our understanding of true discipleship and to align our lives more closely with the heart of God. This 52-day journey has been one of transformation, inviting us to explore what it truly means to live as followers of Jesus Christ.

From the very first day, we were invited to shift our focus from an audience of many to an Audience of One, recognizing that our worth is not measured by the applause of the world but by our faithfulness to God. As Colossians 3:23 reminds us, *"Whatever you do, work at it with all your heart, as working for the Lord, not for human masters."* This theme set the tone for a journey that continually called us to examine the core of our motivations and the sincerity of our faith.

Throughout this journey, we were reminded of the power of the cross and the significance of drawing near to it. The closer we get to the cross, the more we understand the true cost of discipleship—a theme that resonates throughout this devotional. Jesus calls us to a life of sacrifice, faithfulness, and obedience, a call that often stands in stark contrast to the world's definition of success. As we explored the distinction between success and faithfulness, we were challenged to redefine our ambitions in light of God's eternal purposes. As Jesus said in Matthew 16:24, *"Whoever wants to be my disciple must deny themselves and take up their cross and follow me."*

The journey also took us through the essentials of spiritual maturity, urging us to move beyond a superficial understanding of faith to a deep and abiding relationship with God. We explored the vital role of focus in our spiritual lives, learning that a clear vision centered on Christ enables us to navigate life's complexities with wisdom and grace. Hebrews 12:2 encourages us to do this by *"fixing our eyes on Jesus, the pioneer and perfecter of faith."*

We delved into the concepts of reformation and revival, understanding that both are essential to the vitality of the church. While reformation calls us to align our practices and beliefs with biblical truth, revival breathes new life into our spiritual communities, igniting a passion for God's work in the world. Romans 12:2 exhorts us to be transformed by the renewing of our minds, emphasizing the ongoing need for both personal and communal renewal.

The journey also highlighted the importance of leadership and mentorship in the context of discipleship. We saw the power of investing in others, fostering a culture of growth and mutual encouragement. As we seek to grow as leaders, we are reminded that authentic leadership is rooted in humility and service, reflecting the character of Christ. Philippians 2:3-4 guides us to *"do nothing out of selfish ambition or vain conceit. Rather, in humility value others above yourselves, not looking to your own interests but each of you to the interests of the others."*

Each day's reading challenged us to consider the practical implications of our faith. From exploring the dynamics of relationships to understanding the cost of our calling, we were called to integrate these lessons into our daily lives. The questions and reflections at the end of each chapter encouraged us to engage deeply with the material, prompting us to live out our faith with intentionality and purpose, as expressed in James 1:22, *"Do not merely listen to the word, and so deceive yourselves. Do what it says."*

As we reflect on this journey, we are reminded of the importance of community. Discipleship is not a solitary endeavor but a shared journey, one that thrives in supportive and loving relationships. We are called to invest in the lives of others, to learn from those who have gone before us, and to pass on the wisdom we have gained to future generations. Proverbs 27:17 illustrates this beautifully: *"As iron sharpens iron, so one person sharpens another."*

In closing, may this 52-day journey be a source of ongoing inspiration and growth in your life. As you continue on your journey of discipleship, may you be strengthened in your faith, equipped to fulfill your unique calling, and empowered to make a meaningful impact in the world for the glory of God. Let us carry forward the lessons we have learned, living out our faith with authenticity and conviction, and striving to become more like Christ in all that we do. As Ephesians 4:1-2 encourages us, *"I urge you to live a life worthy of the calling you have received. Be completely humble and gentle; be patient, bearing with one another in love."*

Appendices

All content in 52 Days of Discipleship reflects the author's insights and interpretations unless otherwise noted. All referenced Scripture passages are quoted under respective publishers' permissions, as detailed in the copyright section.

Permissions and Copyrights

Excerpts and illustrations drawn from external works are cited in good faith. Notable references include:

Quotes by T.F. Tenney, Jerome Bruner, and others where applicable.

Biblical anecdotes and lessons, adapted from public domain teachings or referenced from recognized Bible translations.

Notes on Cultural or Anecdotal Content

Common stories, such as the Abraham Lincoln anecdote and "spiritual truths better caught than taught" analogy, are presented in alignment with public domain knowledge. If any such materials are recognized as proprietary, updates and attributions will follow standard copyright norms.

Rights and Usage

This book is protected under copyright law. Reproduction of its content, wholly or partially, requires the author's prior written consent unless for brief quotations in reviews or educational contexts.

Acknowledgments

The journey of writing this first of many devotionals has been both inspiring and humbling, and I am deeply grateful to those who have supported and encouraged me on my journey.

First and foremost, I would like to thank my children—Calysta, Zayne, Zion, and Zealynd—for loving their dad through all his imperfections. I will forever thank my beautiful wife, Victoria, for her unwavering love, patience, and understanding throughout my processes.

I am incredibly grateful to the late Bishop Tony Miller, whose guidance and wisdom have profoundly shaped my understanding of discipleship and faith. Thank you for challenging me to deepen my walk with Christ and for being a source of inspiration.

Thank you to Impact Church, Iglesia Vida Nueva, and Discover Life Church for your fellowship and encouragement. Your commitment to living out your faith has been a source of inspiration and has significantly influenced the themes explored in this book.

Finally, I am profoundly grateful to God for His guidance, strength, and inspiration throughout this journey. His presence has been my anchor and motivation in bringing this book to fruition. There is more; the best is yet to come!

To my readers, thank you for embarking on this journey with me. I pray that this devotional will inspire and challenge you to pursue authentic, unadulterated discipleship and deepen your relationship with God.

About The Author

Manny Rivera, alongside his wife Victoria, has been a transformative leader in ministry for over three decades. Together with their spiritual sons and daughters, they have planted three thriving churches and traveled across the globe, speaking at conferences and training leaders in both ministry and marketplace settings. Manny currently oversees these three churches and serves as the Lead Pastor of Discover Life Church in Lawrenceville, Georgia, where his impact continues to ripple through the lives of his congregation and beyond.

Manny's ministry journey began in an unexpected place—a promising career in baseball. However, a life-altering encounter with Jesus radically changed his trajectory, compelling him to step away from baseball and into full-time ministry. Since then, Manny has been driven by a singular passion: to ignite spiritual revival and raise up the next generation of leaders who will carry the fire of the Gospel.

For over 34 years, Manny has devoted himself to training ministry and business leaders through his Timothy Team, a unique discipleship program designed for those seeking to fulfill God's call on their lives. A relentless pursuit of revival, discipleship, and kingdom advancement fuels his leadership. Known for his raw, unfiltered preaching style, Manny's messages are infused with the power of the Holy Spirit, consistently challenging people to live with conviction, purpose, and a deep connection to Christ.

Manny and Victoria are proud parents to four amazing adult children—Calysta, Zayne, Zion (married to Erika), and Zealynd—who continue to inspire them in their walk with God. Manny finds peace and rejuvenation in nature outside of ministry, often hiking and discovering new trails. His love for travel allows him to engage with diverse cultures and bring the message of Christ to the nations, whether he's speaking at international conferences or building relationships across the world.